# wise
## *and*
# *shine*

**Think Clearly, Live Deeply,
Be Someone You Value**

Robert N. Stonehill

WISE AND SHINE: THINK CLEARLY, LIVE DEEPLY, BE SOMEONE YOU VALUE

**Edition 1.0**

ISBN: 978-0578420547

Written by Robert N. Stonehill.

# wise
*and*
## shine

Dedicated to my mother Jean and my friend David.

You live on in my heart.

# acknowledgments

I would like to thank my
biggest cheerleaders: my father
Lloyd, Shawn Michael Sanders,
and Karen Roth for their
encouragement and feedback.
Shawn also helped with the
cover and internal graphics.

I received encouragement
from my family, Sandy Krebs,
Nicholas Yandell, Ilya Egorov,
Davia Larson, Teresa Logan, and
Stoney White.

Many thanks to my editor,
Oriana Leckert.

# Table of Contents

# preface

## *what to expect*

This book presents mental structures that will help you organize your thinking, make deeper connections with people, learn to value yourself and others, and gradually see the big picture. We'll look under the hood to see what the inner world of *being human* means. The book is not complete—how could it be?—but it presents many ideas for how to reimagine our typical daily behaviors.

We'll start with a discussion of who might benefit from this book, who the author is, and how the book is arranged. In Chapter 1, we begin our discussion about empathy. The rest of the book is focused on how to think using wisdom. Wisdom is not omniscience—at least not for us. Rather, wisdom means striving toward better knowledge in the face of uncertainty. It's a type of reflective empathy where we understand the thoughts and feelings of others, *and we are among those others.*

To sort this all out, let us commence.

*Who will benefit from this book?*

This book's dual objectives aim at two main types of people: those interested in finding or pursuing a greater purpose, and those interested in improving their thinking. First, for readers who do not know or follow their purpose, I recommend learning to value others as a part of your personal philosophy. This will give you a clearer understanding of what value *you* bring to the world. If you believe you are a waste of space, you will learn that you are simply listening to the wrong voices. If our culture devalues your gifts, I hope that after reading this book, you will feel empowered to change the culture rather than yourself.

You will learn to value things by new metrics more focused on the power of community. Readers who lack advanced social skills will find some practical advice here. In addition to learning how to deeply connect with people, you will learn new ways to observe and interact with them. You will learn how to learn *from* them. Of course, if you are depressed or otherwise struggling with mental health, do an internet search for a mental health hotline.

Second, creative thinkers, including amateur philosophers and psychologists, will find new ways to theorize and see the world. If you are an open-minded thinker—and thus perhaps a disorganized thinker—this book will help you find new clarity of thought. Rather than explaining all the cognitive biases and mistakes to *avoid* in thinking, we will examine what kinds of thoughts to *pursue*. Creatives will find inspiration here because the imagination is a primary tool of empathy. In mapping out empathy, we simultaneously map out the imagination. Academic theorists can use the organization of the book as a roadmap for their own theorizing. Many of the thinking models we will examine are visual models for categorizing information, and these will lead you to your own new insights.

For thousands of years, the Golden Rule—"Do unto others as you would have them do unto you"— has suffered from under-interpretation. First, many people consider this a childhood rule imposed on us from outside. Why should we be polite to other people? We imagine that this social rule exists to help us all get along better. If we dig a bit deeper, however, we find that people often follow this rule in the hopes of having their kindness reciprocated. That is: do unto others *in order for them to reciprocate* (in the hopes that they will pay you back or return the favor someday). If the mafia boss offers you a favor, one day he will expect something in return. Third, some people who possess empathy and compassion believe that treating others well is a moral obligation, and that practice makes them feel good. These are all correct understandings, but I would like to offer a deeper and more powerful meaning: How we treat other people is usually how we treat *ourselves*.

You could label this perspective as either interconnectedness, bringing the subconscious to light, or subject-object unity—all of which we will cover. Psychologist Carl Jung says, "We have to realize, quite dispassionately, that whatever we fight about in the outside world is also a battle in our inner selves." Before you dismiss this perspective as untrue, consider that some things are *useful for us to think* regardless of their ultimate truth. Another psychologist, William James, tells us that the truth is that which is *useful* to believe.

People who treat others worse than they treat themselves are labeled hypocrites because they practice double standards. They are mean and we shun them, hoping that they will eventually mend their ways. On the other hand, some of you reading this may treat other people *better* than you treat yourself. You must understand that this is also a double standard. You are doing yourself and the world a disservice with this behavior. We will all benefit when you finally show yourself the same respect you show others. So, set a goal of treating people more equally—including yourself. Improving yourself and the world is your new mission.

Now, perhaps the Golden Rule is a goal rather than a truth. However, when you no longer see time as linear, the ideas of goals and truths often merge. For now, in addition to respecting yourself and others, consider aligning the idea of forgiveness to this truth. That is, learn to respect *and forgive* yourself and others. Forgiveness lets you off the hook. It has little to do with the person who is being forgiven.

On the notion of personal growth and improvement, you may disagree with some of the opinions I offer in this book—even though I have avoided offering many. This is as it should be. The book's main agenda is simply to present you with new perspectives that can help you as an individual and lead to a nicer shared human experience. To grow and evolve, one must keep an open mind. To improve your thinking and your life—to WISE AND SHINE—your first principle to consider is intellectual humility.

The underlying premise of this book is that practicing empathy will improve your life and the lives of those around you. Understanding others will help you understand yourself. And nothing will bring you greater satisfaction than striving toward a better world. By practicing empathy, you become the beacon, and the beacon is full of light. Its light shines beyond where you can see.

Technically speaking, wisdom is like empathy combined with what psychologists call 'theory of mind'. If this means little to you, don't panic. Virtually this entire book centers around detailing this concept which includes how to understand people and situations. Understanding is a necessary precursor to caring. While some emotions (e.g. disgust) can be triggered by sensory perceptions rather than thinking, higher-level emotions are the result of higher-level thinking.

This book is neither an essay nor an intellectual argument, but more like a thinking manual. Humanity has outgrown some of its older worldviews, and we need to update or replace our mental models with more sophisticated options. We will preview several of these options in the following chapters. And like choosing from a menu with many delicious dishes, you need not agree with every argument this book makes to enjoy a great dinner at this restaurant.

*Does the author possess credibility?*

Someone advised me to provide a short version of my personal story in order to demonstrate my credibility—to show my life before and after using my own advice, as it were. So, here is a partial story.

I dreaded lunchtime in junior high school. All the four-person tables were invariably full, and nobody wanted me to sit with them. Often, I would skip lunch and hide in the coat closet. In high school, this dreaded lunchtime ritual continued until senior year, when we were allowed to leave the school for lunch. It was not until this final year that I made any friends at all, and certainly not a best friend. Though never intentionally mean to anyone, I was an intellectual snob. I made a girl cry in English class when I questioned a part of her book report presentation. I could not wait to leave my small town and find more interesting people in college.

While at Dartmouth, I became the object of snobbery myself. I was judged based on where I came from, though of course I did not choose to be from Indiana. I slowly realized that in high school I had been judging people on intelligence—expressing my own snobby mentality. I decided then to become un-snobby about everything I could think of. And I stopped prioritizing the importance of intellect.

My pertinent life lesson, then, was a one of inclusion and empathy. That lonely teenage boy still lives somewhere inside me. Snobs exist everywhere, in every political party and institution. People are judged for not having a home, for not having a college degree or PhD, for not being the right skin color. My world has no place for that. I live out the principle of inclusion. I do not ignore people. And this goes for more than just people—it means I remain open to new ideas. Snob mentality and exclusionary clubs that practice cronyism and support one another's pet projects sadden me. But I also believe they are also misguided and missing out. How we treat the weakest in society reflects how we treat ourselves.

I finally made my first best friend when I was twenty years old, and making friends slowly became easier. At age thirty—fifteen years ago—I first discovered spirituality. I especially liked listening to lectures by spiritual teachers Alan Watts and Eckhart Tolle. After achieving enlightenment, I began studying what ancient philosophers as well as contemporary psychologists had to say about the topic of wisdom. Years later, I started a wisdom workshop to teach and discuss what I had learned. My main lesson from spirituality was that intellect only goes so far. It is one tool, and we possess many. Notice how this lesson builds upon the earlier lesson of inclusion.

In my thirties, I began suffering from chronic pain. There is evidence suggesting that trauma and pain can increase empathy, but I would rather be pain-free. My third wisdom lesson was in invisible illness and ableism—where people assume that if you look fine, you must feel fine. Essayist Elaine Scarry writes that our greatest *certainty* in life is how we feel pain. Yet our imaginings of pain within another represents our greatest *doubt*! We cannot assume that other people feel like we do or have been given the opportunities we have. And in the case of invisible illness, we cannot even trust our own eyes to know their struggles.

Whether they are visibly disabled or not, I think one of the main lessons disabled people learn in order to stay sane is that judging other people is all about *intention*. Many able people get surprised by wheelchairs or other physical differences and do not have much experience in dealing with them. But we must be quick to forgive gaffes if the *intentions* are good.

My fourth wisdom lesson was in caring and service. My mother experienced a massive stroke and suffered extensive paralysis. I became one of her caregivers for her final three years. This service was hard and unpleasant on the surface, but it was the most worthwhile thing I had ever done. Our culture barely notices caring as a meaningful endeavor—especially economically—and this is a huge and potentially dangerous mistake. I hope we can all realize, before we ourselves grow old, that we need respect for our elders—and those who take care of them.

My final wisdom lesson was a cold hard truth: we will all die. Everyone you know will die. This is a terrible realization, and there is really nothing sadder in this world. Mourn for a minute—but then realize how much freedom this gives you while you are alive. You are off the hook forever. You are free to do as you please, and the universe has no authority over you. Now, start dancing in the cherry blossoms, because *I* care, and *you* care. You might want to spend more time finding *other* people who care.

In sum, these various discoveries about empathy, inclusion, intention, service, and finality led me to share this book with you. I sincerely hope it will help you shine brightly. Dig deep for a while, learn what you truly want from life—and then start living. Find what gets you out of bed in the morning other than merely habit or duty.

*How is this book organized?*

In Chapter 1, we look at empathy: listening, cooperating, and imagining. Remember, wisdom requires empathy. In Chapter 2, we begin looking at the shapes of thought. Before learning how to use the more complicated shapes, we first learn fundamental building-blocks: the pre-shapes. These include the void, the background, and the single data point. These useful notions are discussed at length, with examples from popular culture.

Chapter 3 introduces binaries. To *transcend* duality, as we say in spirituality, we must first *understand* duality. Chapter 4 extends the discussion of binary systems to examine dialectics and triunes. Dialectics are a well-known concept in Europe, but less so in the United States. Triunes are like triads, popularized by writer Nassim Taleb. We will look at arguments that employ binaries and triunes, and I'll clarify what opposing poles look like. Chapter 5 contains a special case of binary called the "normal curve" or "bell curve". We'll meet Norm—someone we can either imitate or ignore. Norm lives an unexciting life and hides a significant amount of information. Don't let him fool you that he truly exists, because he is imaginary. Binary distinctions beget ever smaller binary distinctions. That is, a normal curve hides tinier normal curves inside it, like a *matryoshka* doll.

In Chapter 6, we finally transcend a binary by envisioning a helix. The oldest symbol of the helix is suggested by the yin-yang, or *taijitu*. More recently, philosophers Georg Hegel and Karl Marx theorize using a helix. Of course, a helix describes DNA, and galaxies too are spirals. We will discuss how the helix informs contemporary thought and helps us visualize change and transcendence. Chapter 7 is the most important chapter for empathic thinking, and features the onion. The layers of an onion represent a host of interesting phenomena, from personal identity formation to the way the learning process works. This popular metaphor has never experienced the kind of investigation we perform here—we use it to explain a wide range of phenomena. Eventually this visualization empowers us to broaden or shrink our circles in accordance with our intentions.

Chapter 8 focuses on matrix thinking. We discuss how our communication is linear while the world itself is not. We thus use matrices to communicate greater information than normal speech or writing allow. Chapter 9 helps us look at the interplay of systems or, in shape-speak, multiple matrices. We all live inside multiple simultaneous systems. Here we explore some of these systems: governments, families, corporations, and more. This overload of information ultimately shows us how uncertainty rules the day, that we should give up the desire to control everything, and that we can never hope to understand it all.

Chapter 10 examines Gestalt perceptions. These are perceptual biases—a topic that I adapt here for social science. These are similar to cognitive biases but have remained somewhat obscure until now. In Chapter 11, we use our knowledge of shapes to czhange the size and shape of the metaphorical iris that focuses our attention. We examine the magic we create by employing different frameworks. Chapter 12 looks specifically at shifting perspectives; we examine how the world appears from the vantage points of other people. Finally, in Chapter 13, we learn to create our own shapes and achieve shapely independence.

We also have a few appendices that did not fit neatly anywhere in the book's body. Appendix A examines wise decision-making. We consider how wise decisions are as much defined by their inputs as by their outcomes. In Appendix B, we manage time and map it to our values, priorities, and goals. Sometimes we neglect the important things in life because we are not managing our schedules in accordance with our values, priorities, and goals. We analyze how to spend our time to better align with what we find important. In Appendix C, we look at integrity in a workbook format, including the various definitions of integrity and how we might pursue a life of integrity. Finally, in Appendix D, we examine humor, looking at humor as the clashing of multiple perspectives. Wisdom often relies on humor.

Schools rarely teach us *how* to think, simply because few researchers study these processes in any systematic way. Few have attempted to map out our internal monologues. Consider this book an early attempt at a new way to organize your thinking. While the subject matter can get pretty heavy, I will try to keep the delivery lighthearted.

The examples draw heavily from psychology and philosophy, but I quote anyone pertinent and insightful—from actor Alan Alda to ancient Chinese philosopher Zhuangzi. Each chapter ends with a review of key points and discussion questions. Please interact with this book. This will not only make the reading experience more enjoyable, it will help you generate your own ideas. Take notes in the margins. Highlight passages you like or—just as importantly—passages you disagree with. Instead of consuming these lessons passively, create a dialogue that can lead you to insights beyond those that the book provides.

# chapter one

## *Witness – Communicate – Imagine*

*Why should we care about other people?*

Let's jump right in. What motivates us to care about other people? To answer this question fully, we must first examine what motivates us to do anything. Beyond our basic needs and instincts for survival, our first rules for behavior come from our parents and guardians. Some of these rules—like always say "please" and "thank you"—are applicable throughout our lives. Other rules—like "don't talk to strangers"—only apply to our earliest years. And of course, we learn many tacit rules simply by observing how our parents and guardians act. Unfortunately, confusion about rules is often a lifelong affair, because no one ever articulates a rule with a caveat like, "This rule is only in effect for the next five years." We'll elaborate on this point in Chapter 8.

Our second main source for behavioral rules is our culture. This source is not entirely separate from our parents, because they of course share in larger cultural values. And as much as some parents attempt to insulate their children, culture encroaches upon them from birth. Even ancient, foreign, or esoteric knowledge is but a few internet clicks away.

As adults, we face a big problem: Cultural messages and norms are diverse and often contradictory. Some rules are law-based, while others are mere suggestions—but sometimes we cannot be certain which is which. We possess the freedom to think for ourselves and choose our own rules for life, but we don't have the time or patience to work everything out from first principles. Thus most of us simply edit the rules that we internalized from our parents and culture.

Let's examine some of the motivations our culture promotes. Certainly the loudest voices tell us that money should be our primary goal. However, most of us quickly learn that this is, at best, incomplete advice. Money can take care of our physical necessities, but it cannot buy happiness far beyond that.

Continuing with the career orientation, quieter voices advise us to find meaningful work. If we start with the assumption that a career is our best path to fulfillment, certainly our careers should be meaningful—at least to *us*. Here we wonder whether we should find the work we *love the most* or whether we should share our greatest *strengths* with the world.

But why should we be defined solely by our jobs? Wiser voices see an even bigger picture. A meaningful life is a product of a work-life balance. Yes, we must find meaningful work, but we must also honor other worthy pursuits. We need to spend time with friends and family, on obligations, hobbies, and rest.

Sometimes we come across a fourth voice that advises us to follow our hearts. Our hearts lead us to various types of work, labors of love, partners, friends, and entertainment. However, this is separate from a life of balance, because the heart is not rational, it is emotional. But do we want to be wholly emotional?

Often the wisest voices are countercultural. These voices are very soft. They tell us that spirituality is the most important thing in the universe. A truly big picture. This is the path for those who seek enlightenment.

Are there any other voices? Do you see anything missing or misleading from this list? All of these goals focus on the self. We seek to serve ourselves. We only have power over ourselves, so how can it be otherwise? If we are individuals, we must act individually. But according to *The Space Between Us* by clinical psychologist Ruthellen Josselson, this view devalues the traditionally "feminine" traits of caring and connection. Rather than focusing upon our individuality, she argues that society is also composed of our intertwined relationships with other people. We can shift our attention and awareness to consider these intertwined relationships as the key unit that makes up our society. In truth, these spaces, or "threads," are where we find the most meaning. Followed to an extreme, we can even imagine the seat of consciousness not in our own heads but in these networks of interconnected minds. We will discuss perspective shifting in different ways throughout this book.

What is the upshot? Should we continue to focus on ourselves, or will we consider giving our relationships more respect? In the end, we care about other people because our connections are where meaning resides. If we only use celebrities as our role models, we get a skewed idea of what is important. Celebrities must be very busy to stay famous, but business is no virtue. We have the opportunity to find more peace and meaning than that—and we should seize it.

*How will practicing empathy benefit us?*

Exploring innovative thinking patterns will help us expand our empathy. Rather than feeling compassion for the sake of mere altruism, let's focus on how practicing empathy can help us find deep meaning. When we expand our empathy, we can benefit from reciprocity. We respect others, and they might respect us. We will certainly become better-liked. But beyond these, we achieve personal benefits. Our own regular practice of empathy delivers: the confidence to live like an independent adult, a deeper understanding of motives, a nuanced sense of creativity or imagination, and deeper connections. Empathy even brings physical benefits. According to James Doty, professor of neurosurgery at Stanford, "As little as two weeks of practicing compassion...can lower blood pressure, boost your immune response and increase your calmness." This compassion practice is accomplished through an intentional focus on our common fears and vulnerabilities, rather than on our respective differences.

By training our minds to see the world from different perspectives, we will gain more power to steer our destinies. The visual metaphors and tools introduced here will help with understanding, but just as important, they are easy to remember. In the upcoming chapters, we discuss various shapes we can incorporate into our thoughts. For example, we will use an onion to demonstrate how to choose our friends, a normal curve to situate our opinions, and a matrix to improve our communications skills.

In essence, our lives are what we spend our time paying attention to. Our thoughts are powerful forces that no one can alter without our permission. Holocaust survivor Viktor Frankl explains it well: "Everything can be taken from a man but one thing: the last of the human freedoms—to choose one's attitude in any given set of circumstances, to choose one's own way." Yet many of us neglect this power. We adopt the thought patterns of people we like or spend time with.

## E is for empathy

According to dictionary.com, "empathy" means "the psychological identification with or vicarious experiencing of the feelings, thoughts, or attitudes of another." For our purposes, we shall abridge this definition: to practice empathy is to identify and understand the thoughts of another. We could perhaps more properly call this "empathic thinking." Traditionally, empathy is painted as an emotional connection to someone else. We envision their struggle and *feel* for them. Indeed, this is the final outcome of empathy. However, in order to reach this goal, we must first *understand*. We must achieve cognition before we can feel emotion. Intellect first, emotion second. While certain emotions may occur to the subconscious, you cannot feel for other people until you intellectually understand them or their predicaments in some fashion. Here we will examine the power of thinking. Instead of the colors of emotion, we will describe the shapes of thought.

Unless we possess telepathy, we can only guess at what other people are thinking at any given moment. We may ask ourselves what beliefs a certain person might hold, what historical circumstances contributed to these beliefs, and how these beliefs might inform their future actions. To learn historical patterns, we could read biographies and ethnographies. But to learn from the present moment, we need different tools.

Practicing empathy using our definition is sometimes called "perspective taking." According to philosopher José Ortega y Gasset, the sum of all the different perspectives on a subject equals the truth, and "the ultimate reality of the world is neither matter nor spirit, is no definite thing, but a perspective." In his mind, the more perspectives we amass within our knowledge, the closer we are to truth. He also equates God with the zero-point where all perspectives balance each other out into nothingness. A very interesting philosophy, no doubt, but practically speaking, it is work enough for us just to examine one different perspective at a time.

Empathy is important to practice for self-knowledge because it allows us to see ourselves from the outside. When we learn information about *other* people, we can see *ourselves* from a new vantage point. If you have ever heard of the Johari window technique, you know that we all exhibit characteristics to others that we ourselves are blind to. One reason to see a psychoanalyst is to add this somewhat impartial perspective to our own knowledge. A talky analyst will explicitly mention our recurring behavioral patterns to help us to discover the root of such behavior. In fact, anytime we ask for feedback in a situation, we are seeking a new perspective that can give us information we ourselves are blind to.

So, while empathy amounts to guessing, we can improve on our guessing abilities. Research from clinical psychologist Helen Riess suggests that empathy is a mutable trait. In other words, we can improve our empathy skills through education and practice. Rather than a mutable trait, I would call empathy simply a process or framework that most people can learn. This book will help with this education, and our daily lives of regular human interaction offer multiple opportunities for practice.

Empathy is wisdom's sibling. The ancient Greeks studied it, then it disappeared for a few thousand years. Until recently, few social scientists approached the study of the various virtues as an actual discipline. Now, however, researchers are tackling empathy in the fields of psychology and philosophy. In psychology, empathy is part of the twenty-year-old positive-psychology movement that researches prosocial traits. Meanwhile, philosophers are studying empathy in the reemerging field of virtue ethics.

Armed with some knowledge of what empathy

means and entails, we now move to preliminary advice on practicing it. The following are direct methods, while the rest of the book focuses more on general practices. These general practices require healthy helpings of imagination. In other words: they're gonna be fun.

*Let's start guessing what other people are thinking!*

How do we begin to form educated guesses about what other people are thinking? As is often the case, we first examine what *not* to do. It can be simplest to articulate negative commandments.

The first rule: do not project. We project when we assume someone else thinks and believes just as we do. While it's safe to assume that other people *possess* thoughts and emotions, actually pinpointing what they are is tricky. Like any cognitive bias, projection runs the gamut from the egregious to the subtle, and it rarely disappears entirely. Our initial aim, then, is to bring awareness to it.

The clearest example of projection that I have ever witnessed occurred while I was at a swimming pool. A young child was running along the edge of the pool, afraid to jump into the water where his father waited. The child kept giggling and screaming: "You're scared! You're scared!" Now, we can infer that the father was not indeed scared; the child was the scared one. The child simply projected his fear onto his father.

Meanwhile, a subtle example of projection occurs when we offer unrequested advice. We usually pull advice from our own experience, but rarely do two different situations perfectly align, and even when they do, we cannot fully know another person's values, priorities, and goals. As film producer Baz Luhrmann tells us, advice is recycled experience "sold for more than it is worth". In other words, we should not emulate the proverbial monkey who tried to save a fish from drowning by placing it on a tree branch. Likewise, if we presume to speak for other people, we had better know exactly what they want us to say. We might also avoid baby-talk and elder-speak as disrespectful projections. Strive to meet people at their eye level and speak to them authentically.

To bypass the pitfalls of projection, we need better ways to engage in perspective taking. Luckily there are many. Over the course of this book, we will discuss various imaginative methods, but the surest antidote to projection is radical listening.

*What is radical listening?*

Listening is a tough job—so difficult, in fact, that the word has ceased to mean what it is intended to mean. We now say "radical" listening to describe a wholly focused attention upon what another person is saying. If you have ever engaged in radical listening, you know it's exhausting. Any virtuous act is. Radical listening requires effort—it's not synonymous with waiting for your turn to speak. If you jump into a conversation with rehearsed lines pulled from a script, you are acting rather than connecting, performing rather than creating.

Media mogul Oprah Winfrey has interviewed

9

thirty thousand people in her career. She is a master listener. One common theme she observes is that, regardless of the topic at hand, people want the validation that comes from *feeling heard*. If we could always remember this underlying need, arguments would become such pleasant affairs! In many cases, the arguments would disappear in puffs of smoke.

When we offer this kind of validation to people, we begin to resolve problems for mutual gain. Instead of competing to be the loudest or most strident in our opinions, we create an enjoyable connection by cooperating with another person. Who doesn't want that? Learning how to offer the validation that comes from truly listening to another person is a subject that deserves its own book, but like many of the ideas here it only gets a few lines. Nowadays we can all use search engines to learn more about any subject.

The actor Alan Alda, another famous interviewer, approaches listening with humility and curiosity. He explains: "Ignorance was my ally as long as it was backed up by curiosity." In kinesthetic attention, instead of listening for spoken cues, we look more deeply at body language. In teaching empathy to scientists, Alda introduces them to the art of improvisation. He compares good communication to good improvisation: creating interaction on the fly without working from a script. In other words, typical acting is not the same as improvisation. Improvisational comedy is engaging to an audience (and a participant) precisely because it is unpredictable. You must observe other people and join them in an activity that makes sense as a whole. If they are miming, for example, you must carefully observe their body language to understand what is transpiring.

If you are practicing radical listening or improvisation, what you hear will always influence how you respond. Both acts take effort, but like any skills, they improve with practice. Both of these skills connect you directly to the person standing—or sitting—in front of you.

*How else can we empathize?*

Empathy is not limited to understanding the people in our immediate vicinity. For example, the great appeal of literature is not pure escapism but the wonder of inhabiting a new world as a new person—a kind of vicarious enjoyment. Indeed, we can use our imaginations to not only become different humans but to pretend we are aliens, animals, plants, or even mossy boulders.

In Camelot, Merlin helped King Arthur learn empathy by transforming him into various animals. As a bird, he could observe the world from above—a literal bird's-eye view. Ecologists, too, often look for wisdom in the natural world. For example, we can gain wisdom by pondering the philosophy of an old tree: stay rooted but respond appropriately to the changing seasons.

The characters we inhabit in this book will be strange creatures—shapes that present new ways to think about the world. These imaginary shapes are our guides to challenge and change our thinking. We can spend a lifetime learning new information, but if we never change *how* we think or the way we form opinions, what exactly have we learned?

Before we meet our shapely empathy gang, we need to organize our own minds a bit. We now take a shallow dive inward to observe what—if anything—is in there.

*The chaotic inner world*

Imagine yourself in a huge warehouse filled with boxes. The boxes are large and small, long and short, old and new—some you have not opened in decades, and some you have *never* opened. Some of the boxes that you use every day have toppled onto their sides, strewing their contents across the floor. This is your true life in here, amid the boxes. It's your inner world, and it requires some reorganization.

Very few people venture to describe their inner lives, which is quite surprising, since we spend so much of our time there! If your inner life is anything like mine, it's pretty chaotic: thoughts, emotions, and sense perceptions all competing for immediate attention. "It's a warm evening. That wind is a bit chilly. I wonder if I should put on a sweater. Oh, I love this sweater! I bought it with my best friend at my favorite store. It feels so soft." One thought rarely finishes itself before a second grabs the spotlight. While we can never fully escape this stream of consciousness, our empathy tools will provide us with some useful roadmaps to both clarify and tame these inner hurricanes.

Also called "metacognitive strategies," our empathy tools help us address such topics as how to form better opinions, how strongly to hold various opinions, and how we might better align our values with our goals and actions. Returning to the warehouse metaphor, we will open up all of our boxes, tag the inventory, and arrange everything to work for us. When we work to harness our thoughts, eventually it becomes easier to wrangle our emotions as well.

*What motivates us to think?*

To better organize our thoughts, we need to know what leads us to think in the first place. What makes our inner worlds so chaotic? Our thoughts usually appear in our minds as sentence fragments or images—general or specific, concrete or abstract, emotional or informational. While many of us allow our thoughts to remain murky and unexplored, we can all better organize our minds. Like any pursuit, this involves attention and dedication. In fact, we pay so little attention to organizing our inner lives that with one hour of practice each week, we could all make tremendous strides.

Physicist and philosopher L.L. Whyte observes that a thought arises the moment we encounter a problem. This problem-centered approach to thinking is both intentional and productive. For example, we come upon a closed door and know that to open it we must turn the knob. More elaborate problems simply require more thought. With this kind of thinking, we eventually build rocket ships and send them to the moon. Or if we don't like the heat, we invent the air conditioner.

A second type of thinking is unintentional and can be either productive or unproductive. We usually call it worry. Worry is like sunshine: a small helping gives you Vitamin D, while a large helping gives you the Big C. When you worry just a bit, you increase your adrenaline and thus your performance. But if you worry too much, your thoughts will imprison and torture you, spinning scenarios around in your head without end. Such fretting is counterproductive and addictive but quite common. Sometimes we call this kind of fretting "negative self-talk."

The final type of thinking is intentional yet unproductive—at least if you're angling for immediate results. This kind of thinking is philosophical. While many consider philosophy impractical, philosophical thoughts can change the world as much as any new technology. We need look no further than Adam Smith or Karl Marx to find philosophers with a worldwide and lasting impact.

Of course, more achievable than changing the outer world is changing the inner world. We can change our minds about life, look at things with new attitudes, and rewrite our own personal philosophies. Indeed, we all think and act from personal philosophies, whether unexamined, tacitly acknowledged, or well defined. In philosophy, we can engage in meta-thinking, which is thinking *about* thinking. We employ meta-thinking when we strategize, plan our time, or attempt to align our values with our goals.

The moment we think, we separate ourselves from the outside world and sever our ties to the social world. This brings both advantages and disadvantages.

*The ups and downs of intentional thought*

There are, of course, many advantages to actively choosing our thoughts. The main advantage of our intentional, internal thoughts is that we are the rulers of our inner realms. We decide what goes on. We are the dictators, queens, and kings. We are free from distraction in a secret garden where we can take time to ponder and imagine whatever we want. We become immune to the outside world. We can press the secret "bliss" button. We can filter every outside experience through thought. Most importantly, thought lies at the leading edge of creation. We can feel, breathe, eat, and love without thought—but we cannot create new worlds without it. In this book, we will take advantage of the separation of our thoughts from reality. We will allow our imagination to reach its full potential. The imaginary shapes we study are tools that will help us when we finally return to the social world. We need tools because the world is a very complicated place.

Our greatest assets often perform double duty as our greatest liabilities. Similarly, our thinking can offer us great strength or become a great weakness. In other words, we can use our thoughts to change our world for better or for worse. Thoughts can be creative or destructive. When we live inside a world of reactionary thoughts, for example, we cede our power to other people. Each passerby can wrest control from us depending upon what they say or do. They can infuriate us with behavior we don't like or gladden us with a sincere smile. Do you really want to be at the mercy of every person you encounter?

A further disadvantage of intentional thought is that our thoughts can never reach the complexity of reality, meaning they do not correspond perfectly with the outside world. They are rife with generalizations, exaggerations, and biases. Anything we can imagine is merely a weak shadow when compared to its real counterpart.

We seek to understand the world but cannot. While our minds are large compared to those of the other animals, the universe is still larger—and growing. New complications arise every single day. We do not possess adequate brainpower either as individuals or in repository as a species to comprehend a growing universe. And the continual progression of time can make such knowledge stale when we finally wish to retrieve it.

In sum, in order to supplement our understanding of the world, we use knowledge coupled with imagination. Imagination allows us to gain knowledge from things we have not personally experienced. Both education and the experiences of other people bring us knowledge that is heavily laden with imagination. And in the end, all empathy stems from the imagination.

*Why does thinking present such a struggle?*

We struggle with thinking for several reasons. First, according to Aristotle, humans inhabit a hybrid, or "between," state. Our feet are in the clay and our heads are in the clouds. In other words, human existence combines animal instinct with consciousness: the ability to think independently. As such, our desires go beyond mere survival. Aristotle's prescription for correct action in such a situation calls for a middle path known as the Golden Mean—the halfway mark between any two extremes. This theory is very problematic, however, because we can augment or diminish any action, regardless of where it sits on a continuum. Thus, if the endpoints are not fixed, neither is a midpoint. Without certain endpoints of excess or scarcity, midpoints—and thus guideposts—are impossible to find.

Second, in addition to life in this hybrid state between the clay and the clouds, we arise through a process of evolution that does not prioritize human happiness. In fact, survival is our goal, while happiness is largely irrelevant to the survival of the species. According to evolutionary theory, humans are often competitive at the individual level but cooperative at the group level. Of course, it's even more complicated than this when we separate into multiple tribes. When our very genetics pull us in two different directions at once, mental chaos is inevitable.

Third, we possess subconscious desires that sometimes conflict with our best interests. Freud explains how our id, ego, and superego are often at war with one another. In Freud's schema, we are pulled in three different directions. We have the animal instincts, the self, and the internalized parent or authority figure to choose from.

Fourth, we are reflective. This means that, in addition to how we might act naturally, we take our cues from education and other people. When an economist tells us that we tend to behave in a certain way, for example, we can react by behaving exactly thus, or we can revolt and consciously choose the opposite behavior just to be difficult. The theories of economics that usually enter public discourse tend to promotes the idea of our selfish natures. Some economists study cooperation, but they are perhaps not as loud. Likewise, the traditional field of ethics focuses on doing the *least harm*, rather than the *most good*. Slowly people are addressing this omission, but tradition often holds great power.

Recently the fields of psychology and philosophy have begun studying prosocial and cooperative behavior. Positive psychology examines our competitiveness turned inward in the form of self-improvement: we compete with our former selves rather than against other people. This is important research. Unfortunately, many of the findings also suggest that prosocial behaviors present a cost to the individual practicing them. If our culture does not value traits like empathy or honesty, the prosocial person barely receives any attention at all.

Finally, in order to think, we need focused attention and to be free of distraction, but what we attend to is easily countermanded by out instincts. Our evolutionary heritage forces us to heed things that stand out in our environment—the nonconformities—as these often alert us to danger. Sometimes the nonconformities are threats, but more often than not, they are just different people passing by. In sum, our thoughts pull us in multiple directions through multiple priorities, and we possess evolutionary tendencies that we can never fully escape.

In the following chapters, we will meet the shapes, frames, and angles that will help us deepen and broaden our empathy. We will use various thinking tools to harness the power of perspective shifting. While *what* we think may be context-dependent, *how* we think does not have to be. As you read through the book, I hope you will grow to love these shapes—these characters of the imaginary world—as much as I do. My personal favorite is the matrix because it allows us to empathize with aliens. If you prefer a different shape, let me know! I practice radical availability and would love to talk with you about shapes all day.

One final note before we begin: While thought permeates our inner lives, there is much more to life than thinking. On her 110$^{th}$ birthday, Flossie Dickey, when asked the secret to her long life, answered, "I don't fight it, I just live it." Let us plaster these words to the backs of our minds, even as we learn how truly powerful thought can be.

*Key Ideas*

- We learn rules from our parents and culture, but we need not obey childish rules into adulthood, nor cultural rules that we disagree with.

- Our culture focuses on the self rather than on the relationships in which we find meaning.

- We help ourselves by practicing empathy.

- Our thoughts are our own property, but we often neglect their power.

- Interacting with this book will make reading it more meaningful.

- Empathy is similar to perspective-taking.

- Empathy is a mutable trait that we can improve through education and practice.

- We should be wary of projection.

- Good listening is like improvisation: what you hear impacts what you say next.

- We can use our imaginations to practice empathy.

- Our inner worlds are often chaotic.

- Thinking can be intentional/unintentional and productive/unproductive.

- Thoughts can change our worlds for better or for worse.

- Reality is more complex than any thought can be.

- Priorities and evolutionary tendencies pull our thoughts in different directions.

- Remember, there is more to life than thought.


*Discussion Questions*

- What are some thinking tools we commonly use?

- What are some additional situations that pull our thoughts in multiple directions?


*Suggested Activities*

- Practice listening to someone.

- Engage in an improv session.

- Read about Freud's separation of the mind into three parts: id, ego, and superego. Relate this to Aristotle's schema.

- Look at a photograph and describe what you see to another person who cannot see the photograph. Consider how long it takes them to get even a tiny bit of the conveyed information correct.

# chapter
# two

*The Planet of the Pre-Shapes*

*Overview*

A good education helps us get what we want, while a transformative education helps us *change* what we want. Change can be scary, but we should not fear those changes brought on by growth and improvement. If we seek to grow, we must embrace change—we must stay open-minded enough to consider new ideas. The best way to rebuild our attitudes is from the ground up. Similarly, our empathy shapes require certain fundamental building blocks to attain their full significance. In this chapter, we explore the power of attitudes and creativity, and we look at the first principles behind the construction of our empathy shapes.

As we stress throughout this book, we must learn about people before we can care about them—and this includes ourselves. This is why reflection and emotional education are critical. When we learn a new language, we open our minds to a new culture. Along with the language, we learn new values, new ways of life, and new perspectives on the world. In this book we present a new language: the language of imaginary shapes. This language will help you clarify your thoughts. When we learn a language as an adult, we begin with the building blocks of that language: the alphabet. While some foreign language teaching methods begin with the rote memorization of basic phrases, adults can rarely achieve fluency in a language without knowing the alphabet.

Here we will learn the alphabet to help us later understand the empathy shapes. We'll uncover some hidden ideas that underlie shapes and learn about three fundamental notions that I like to call pre-shapes: the void, the background, and the single data point. (Hi, Dottie!)

*What are pre-shapes?*

Like embryonic shapes, pre-shapes form the building blocks of familiar shapes, but we would not call them fully developed. They are crucial, however: without them there could be no shapes. While you already know some of the characteristics of these pre-shapes, you have probably never seen them organized like this. I will always try to provide new information when I rehash common knowledge. Tying our common knowledge to new ideas helps promote understanding.

Our empathic embryonic shapes are neither simple nor easy to understand. In fact, they are quite impossible to fully comprehend, and that's okay. We can live without certainty. In fact, when we learn to appreciate the notion of uncertainty, perhaps we can begin to reconsider a great many other ideas we hold firmly.

Just as Genesis begins with a discussion of the void, we adhere to this ancient template. The void is probably the most fundamental concept underlying the universe. Indeed, the void predates the Big Bang—though some might argue that the Big Bang precipitated the void.

*What is the void?*

The void exists everywhere and nowhere at the same time. It is imaginary yet real. It contains many paradoxes and is difficult to think about. By definition, a void is the absence of a *thing*. While the void is not fully comprehensible to us, we understand aspects of it through simile and metaphor. If we take a visual example like a painting, the foreground would be the paint and the background would be the blank canvas, while the absence of the paint *and* canvas would be the void.

In spoken communication, the void manifests as silence. When we examine silence, we learn how much it actually communicates. In a conversation, silence can signal that a message has not been heard. It can mean a message is being digested. Silence can signal respect, defiance, or solidarity with silent others. Silence can express disappointment, rejection, or politeness. Silence can signal the end of a speech or the prompt for another person to speak. However, silence outside of a communication is a void from which all speech originates.

25

A void cannot contain parameters. Thus, a zero is often not the same as a void. To be more precise with semantics, an empty room is not a void because it contains space. Space is itself a thing rather than a no-thing. However, this metaphor is how we typically understand the meaning of the void.

A true void (that is also devoid of any context) does not exist anywhere that we can normally comprehend. A void is thus *imaginary*. Yet we can feel and sense the void, and it is very real, even if we cannot directly apprehend it through our sense perceptions. In spirituality, some people might call this the Source or God. All of the world that we see springs from this Source. The word is less important than the concept.

*How can something imaginary be important?*

When we are small, we often have great imaginations. As we age, we tend to imagine less, and we turn our focus to more practical matters. However, if you have ever read *The Little Prince*, you might remember that imaginary things are the *most* important. As Antoine de Saint-Exupéry writes, "Our eyes cannot see the important things. It is only with the heart that we can see them clearly." So what kinds of things do we see with the heart? Love, friendship, and justice come to mind. As Plato wrote, we see reality as the flicker of shadows upon the walls of a cave. In other words, we do not see *anything* in its truest form. This is doubly true for the things we value most, like empathy and wisdom. If we agree that we are made up of mind, body, and spirit, we usually agree that our spirits are invisible to the naked eye.

Recent scientific research suggests that our brains barely distinguish between the real and the unreal. Positive affirmations can help turn around a negative mindset because our brains listen to what we tell them. It does not matter whether the things we say are literally true. (In fact, nothing we say is *literally* true, but that is for a later discussion.)

Our beliefs create our reality. Yes, things happen to us, but our reactions to events are largely within our control. If we were to readily perceive fictional characters as unreal, then consuming TV shows and novels would totally lose its allure.

Our brains also possess mirror neurons for *imagined* empathy. Mirror neurons copy the behaviors we observe in other people, whether they are real people or those in paintings or books. For example, when we see a photo of an overcrowded scene, we begin to feel claustrophobic. In an extreme case, then, we can create a work of art and control how we think and feel about it. This means that we have the ultimate power to change our thoughts and emotions.

*What power does the void offer us?*

The void is both extremely compelling and downright scary. We need to be careful when we tap into the power of the void. When we encounter a void, we must pay close attention to how we intend to fill it. We can fill it with negative nasties like harmful addictions, or we can add more freedom and abundance to our lives. The primary power of the void lies in its creative potential. Indeed, it is pure potential—the wellspring and source of all creativity.

We often divide artistic and creative works into two general categories: ideas that rearrange old material, or ideas that are mostly fresh. Of course, most artistic works fall between these two extremes, but often we either complain that an idea is "too derivative" or we exclaim, "Wow, I never thought of that!" The extreme endpoints of this continuum rarely exist—nothing is entirely a recycled idea. Nothing is entirely without precedent—except perhaps for *Planet of the Apes*. Often expertise in a specific field is required to create or judge this dichotomy. Even so, artists are usually long dead before people start to consider their works ground-breaking.

Imagine the case of film critics who have seen thousands of movies. They eventually tire of stock characters and familiar situations. Something original will entice them. They will seemingly award extra stars for creativity. A critic's favorite films are thus more likely to be less popular or too experimental for mainstream tastes. In fact, sometimes the lack of appeal to mainstream tastes sparks the expert's interest in the first place!

Creativity requires the void because it *fills* the void. The same holds true for our inner lives—our thoughts and opinions about the world. Without some empty space around our thoughts and opinions, there is no room for them to grow and change. If you want to learn something new, you have to prepare a space for it. After we have prepared some space, we call ourselves open-minded. We can easily practice this mindset. The next time someone asks your opinion on a topic, tell them you do not have one—that you are still weighing the facts. You have *voided* your old opinion and will revisit the topic later. This method bends the void to our own purposes. Such a practice will put you in good company: Socrates practiced a similar approach and was considered the wisest man in Athens. And depending on your typical attitude, your new behavior might even stun your friends.

We can use the void to create buffer zones in our thoughts and beliefs. This is a very popular topic in spirituality, especially as discussed by Eckhart Tolle. Specifically, we create space between the outside world and our reactions to it. Mastery of this practice allows us to become authentic creators of our own lives, rather than the mere sum of our reactions to other people and other things. When we take this to its extreme, we dis-identify from the outside world and all material things. (We'll learn more about this behavior in a later chapter when we meet the empathic onion.)


*How does one create a buffer?*

A buffer is a gap, a shield, a moat, a form of body armor. We can create imaginary buffers around our inner lives and strengthen these buffers with practice. An ascetic monk, for example, works endlessly to master this art.

We create buffers through sheer willpower or conscious effort. The two main types of imaginary buffers are time buffers and space buffers. A time buffer provides us with a time lag so that we can process our environment at our own pace. This is a very vulnerable position; hence, people interested in this practice often attend spiritual retreats. You cannot imagine time lags while you are stuck in traffic or amid busy people demanding your undivided attention.

To create a time buffer, simply react to things more slowly than usual. Each time a stimulus in your environment provokes a reaction in your thinking, don't make a snap judgment about it. In other words, refrain from immediate reaction.

In psychoanalysis, a patient repeatedly examines the arrow that leads from stimulus to behavior. Often our first reactions to events are based on habits— sometimes from as far back as our childhoods. With advancing age, of course, these habitual reactions rest upon outdated premises. Sometimes our reactions rest instead upon false premises. We must remember to change our internal compass without changing our outer reality. Bringing outdated reactions to light allows us to modify them. The time buffer works as a tool that slows down the arrow leading from environment to inner world. We cannot observe objects and processes that move at lightning speed, so we slow them down to where we can study them—much like a slow-motion replay in sports.

time           time

stimulus $\longrightarrow$ thought $\longrightarrow$ response

space          space

Imagine walking down the sidewalk when a lawn sprinkler suddenly takes aim and sprays you with water. How do you respond? Your immediate response might be anger, but let's use a time buffer. If you slow down the reaction arrow, you probably discover that the initial response is *surprise* followed by anger. Now we're getting somewhere! We can work with surprise, because surprise is less judgmental. As a surprise is neither good nor bad in itself, take this feeling of surprise and imagine new and different trajectories for it. For example, if we are strolling on a hot day, the sprinkler cools us off. If we are walking to a job interview, the sprinkler provides an interesting anecdote to share. In any case, the sprinkler merely followed its program. It did not consciously betray us—it lacks any motivation at all. We choose to react the way we do. So rather than get mad, we can simply choose to laugh.

A space buffer, on the other hand, is an elongation of the *area* between a stimulus and a response. In other words, you stretch out the many steps of a process to better examine them. With more practice using time and space buffers, we begin to observe how closely time and space are related!

Since this is an imaginary game, you can choose either time or space as your buffer. What other types of buffers might help this process? Certainly silence can be a helpful buffer. You can choose whatever type of buffer works best for you.

In sum, use the void to create, to open your mind, or to buffer your inner world. Remember that in the book of Genesis, God created the world from the void because He was lonely. Before we too get lonely, let's move on to explore the second pre-shape: the background.

*What is a background?*

A background always goes out to lunch with its foreground friend attached at the hip. Like twins, they need one another, even as they vie for our attention. The segment of a scene that we focus our attention on is the foreground. The part we ignore—the periphery—is the background. Sometimes the context of a situation is the background. How much attention we pay to backgrounds differs by individual and by culture, but we could all use further training in examining them.

You will find that a lot of great people and things inhabit backgrounds. The extras in a movie who make a scene realistic move in the background. The technicians and writers of movies work in the background. The unknown wife who enabled her husband's greatness lives in the background of history. Minorities of all sorts live in the background. Do you live in the background? I certainly do. Though I am an extrovert, not many people know me.

How do we lose sight of all these great stories? Our evolutionary heritage—and thus our instinct for survival—prioritizes safety, so we continually scan our environment and focus on certain points. Do not think of this in purely visual terms. All of our sense organs play a role: sight, sound, smell, touch, and sometimes taste. (Although rarely do we *taste* danger—more likely, danger tastes *us*.) Visually speaking, certain objects come more naturally to our attention: moving objects, colorful objects, odd objects, and unfamiliar objects. Because our sense perceptions are often very trustworthy, we tend to carry their information too far, into more abstract and intellectual domains. This causes many cognitive biases. While we might never completely avoid cognitive biases, we can at least bring awareness to them.

In addition to checking for potential danger, we also notice potential friends. Dogs notice other dogs, children notice other children, and minorities of every type often notice other minorities. In fact, when we learn a new word, we often come across it repeatedly. While word usage does trend and cycle, this phenomenon is more likely the result of our newly attuned attention. The law of attraction, a popular spiritual framework, tells us that "like attracts like." This is true, even while science teaches us that opposites attract. Indeed, both are true.

We now turn to the field of literary criticism. Philosopher Jacques Derrida popularized deconstruction, a method to amplify the background of a text. For example, whenever a text holds one particular claim in esteem (the foreground), the text must implicitly hide or devalue another view, which it backgrounds. In fact, words do not possess inherent meaning but only create meaning through contrast with other, different words. Thus, for example, "being" only makes sense in contrast with "nothingness"—its opposite.

The deconstruction method has obvious political implications, and political theorist Karl Marx elucidated them. Marx argued that the working classes—the background—are the losers in a capitalist system that foregrounds capital. Marx built his ideas upon philosopher Georg Hegel, who built upon ancient Chinese philosopher Laozi. These ideas are not new but forever remain revolutionary.

In addition to the contexts of sensory organs, literature, philosophy, and politics, where do we find backgrounds? People have backgrounds! In this case, we mean histories. (If a person's history is their background, what is their foreground?) Finally, life backgrounds grounds death.

How do we use this knowledge? One idea is to train our attention to foreground things in succession. This practice helps us observe background elements that we rarely notice.

*So how do I use backgrounds?*

If you create something—and we all do—then you understand backgrounds. Every creative endeavor requires a background of some sort. For example, good storytellers build background information to shape their characters and settings. Injecting good background information leads to verisimilitude, or believability. If you have never visited Russia but you presume to write a story based there, someone astute will notice your mistakes. In mediocre fiction, a writer will describe a character's background through narration. In good fiction, characters will let slip hints about their backgrounds. This is how a reader gets to know a character. If a real person without a background moves in next door, people quickly assume things and let their imaginations run wild, even if it is none of their business.

Our own backgrounds are crucial, but not because they define us. They don't. Rather our experiences speak to the vagaries of life. For example, we cannot be happy if we have never known sadness—and we certainly will not be thankful for our happiness. Indeed, without contrast, we could not understand anything at all. Imagine the pages of this book without the whitish paper (or screen) behind them. You would be hard-pressed to read anything! Contrast is important not for us to judge things, but to make sense of things.

Important with respect to empathy, and a situation that people often overlook, is that you cannot win a race without other contestants. You need the slower contestants—the so-called losers—or there could be no race in the first place. You have to win *against* someone—even if that someone is you. If you run your "personal best" time, you've won against your older self. Some situations, of course, acknowledge this fact much better than others. If you win something, therefore, be sure to thank everyone for participating and *for making it possible*.

We can consciously change what we pay attention to in life. We can foreground certain things and background others. We do not have to stick to default settings. Start today by making a new assumption about something important, and follow where it leads. Focus on something you usually find insignificant and find out why it might be important. When you look at a family photograph, try looking at someone other than yourself. In fact, try looking at the background. You might find something interesting and worthwhile.

35

We now turn to our third pre-shape, Dot.

*Who or what is Dottie?*

Meet Dottie, our third and final pre-shape. Dottie feels all alone in the world—because she is. Visualize her as a speck of data on a background, in the void. Dottie teaches us about the interdependence of everything. After that discussion, we'll examine how to use her in the incremental approach to life. Finally, we'll briefly discuss the act of labeling.

Imagine that Dottie is something tiny, like a paramecium—a one-celled organism. Even something so tiny needs something to eat and somewhere to live. It cannot exist in total isolation. We often think of ourselves as closed shapes of skin moving around in the world. Yet we are completely embedded within our environments. Without air, we would suffocate. Without food, we would starve. Outside of a very limited band of temperature, we would freeze or boil. In fact, we could not describe a human to an alien without also explaining how we interact with our environment. Alan Watts thus calls us "organism-environments."

Furthermore, as social animals, we depend upon many other people for our existence. Of course, we have our parents who gave us life, but we also live in communities where we trade with other people using a complex bartering system.

Since everything is interconnected, we can never *fully* understand anything, because we would have to explain not only it, but all the interconnections that give it meaning. As cosmologist Carl Sagan said, "To bake an apple pie from scratch, we must first create the universe." There are things we comprehend quite well, but these things do not tend to be our thoughts about the world. Our certainty is reserved more for inner truths. For example, we are certain when we are in physical pain, and we are certain when we are in love. Neither of these examples is a mere thought.

*What is the incremental approach to life?*

Now envision Dottie as a link in a chain. A single link is quite worthless, but if we bring several links together, we create a chain, and thus a powerful tool. This is a good metaphor for teamwork, but here we will look at it from the perspective of time.

As Laozi writes, the journey of a thousand miles begins with a single step. No matter how big your goal or how short your time, you can always find a dot of time to work toward a goal. If you do something for only one minute a day, you will spend six hours per year on that thing. When you are young, you might think a year is a long time, but eventually you will realize it is short. I urge you to begin working toward your loftiest goals with this mindset. Our lives are lived one moment at a time.

Finally, Dottie teaches us an introductory lesson about labeling. Two monks were sitting on a hillside passing the afternoon away when one of them looked up and pointed, saying: "They call that a tree." Both monks laughed. The humor, to them, was in the reduction of something as magnificent as a tree into the short little word "tree."

A tree is an amalgam—a combination of smaller parts. We use amalgams all the time—maybe too often. A tree has many parts, and every tree is unique. Yet we tend to think with the mention of the word "tree" that we somehow understand what a tree is. But naming something is not the same as understanding it. Humans are amalgams of various organs, most of which must work or we would not survive. Yet we do not even pretend to understand everything happening in our bodies, let alone our minds.

In sum, we can use the void, the background, and Dottie in our thinking. They are visual metaphors and memory aids. Sometimes we can think better in shapes than in words. In the next chapter, we'll turn to the concepts of binary and duality.

*Key Ideas*

- Growth requires change, so to grow we must be open to change.

- We should become comfortable with uncertainty.

- The void is the absence of language, smell, object, etc.

- The real, the imagined, and the invisible are all parts of our most meaningful reality.

- The void is pure potential for creativity.

- We can create time and space buffers.

- Backgrounds are essential yet underappreciated because of our culture and evolutionary heritage.

- We can foreground things in succession.

- We are interconnected with our environment.

- Consider the incremental approach to life where we live one moment at a time.

- Be careful with labels.


*Discussion Questions*

- What other kind of buffers can we use in addition to time and space?

- How can we pay more attention to backgrounds?

- Why do we often fail to see how interconnected we are?

*Suggested Activities*

- Enter the void. But be sure to come back with something new.

- Examine the backgrounds in some photographs or of some fictional people.

- Think of a long-term goal that you can work on for one minute per day.

# chapter three

## Binary and Duality – Justice and Symmetry

*Overview*

In the last chapter, we examined the world of voids, backgrounds, and single data points. We now progress to ideas surrounding the number two. The number two is quite fundamental to our universe. Two is the number we get when we add one and one, of course, but we can also make two when we divide one in half! That is, we can clone one to make two, or we can divide it in half to obtain two halves. When we want to discuss the number two, we often use the following words: twin, double, couple, dyad, duet, binary, duel, and dual. In this chapter, we look at the number two and focus specifically upon the ideas of binary and duality. The idea of binary often ties into computing and decision-making, while the idea of duality often loiters near the spirituality talk of yin and yang.

## Binary in black and white

A binary system is one that contains exactly two elements. For example, in astronomy, a binary system is a solar system with two suns. In electronics, the two binary elements are *off* and *on*, symbolized by zero (0) and one (1). You may even notice these two symbols on some power switches. At their most fundamental level, all computer systems are simply transistor sets that switch between *off* and *on*. When we combine enough of these transistors together, the system becomes quite powerful. Contemporary computers hide their binary guts through graphical user interfaces and programming languages that are shortcuts to manipulating these low-level binary operations.

The oldest known source of a binary system is the Chinese I Ching, also known as *The Book of Changes*, dating back more than three thousand years. Mathematician Blaise Pascal was quite fascinated with the I Ching, and there exists a computer programming language named after Pascal, so you can see how closely the new and old connect in the idea of binary.

Binaries do more than permeate our world—they actually compose a fundamental aspect of it. Imagine a coin with only one side. More importantly, imagine trying to read a page that is either all black or all white. It is only by the contrast of the printing and the background colors that we can see anything at all on the page.

Binaries are powerful, but they can become problematic when they creep into our social constructions, such as concepts like marriage, which do not exist in nature but which we adhere to all the same. In sociological circles, cutting-edge thinkers warn us to avoid binary thinking, as it is reductionist. Reduction may be fine for cooking a sauce or generalizing ideas, but it is rude and sometimes dehumanizing to reduce living people to labels or simplistic categories.

Binaries are easy to create. For example, do matter and energy exist in waves or in particles? Einstein's equation $E = mc^2$ shows how matter transforms into energy, implying that they are but two sides of the same coin. We could also think about matter and energy as units and processes. The categorization of things into units and processes presents considerable difficulty because it often boils down to mere matters of taste.

I posit further that the world consists of units, processes, and *ideas*. If we exist in an open system, ideas represent the necessary meta-perspective leading to ideas about ideas *ad nauseum* to create an infinite loop. If you want to engage in some fun ideation, think about some things you generally consider to be matter and look at them as sets of actions instead. Rinse, reverse, and repeat.

*More about binary*

Binary is a system or world of two. Ironically, or perhaps counterintuitively, this system of two does not contain the actual digit 2 but consists of only 0 and 1. We can, of course, represent the concept of two, which is written in binary notation as 10.

We use a decimal system perhaps because we possess ten fingers. In post-revolution France, there were short-lived attempts to decimalize calendars and days in order to unify our numbering systems, but these experiments did not catch on.

Using the digits 0 and 1 is not a mandatory rule of binary systems; it simply evolved in the computing context. A binary decision is any decision between two different options. For computers, these two different options are "electricity on" or "electricity off." Thus, the two options are called 0 and 1, where 0 means *off* and 1 means *on*. This makes more intuitive sense than using 1 and 2 in our binary system. In other words, the existence of a current is represented as 1, and the lack of a current is 0. To build a system from this very basic rule, we simply stack one transistor onto another. Each additional transistor doubles the number of decisions the computer can process. With enough transistors, the computer can process millions of complex decisions.

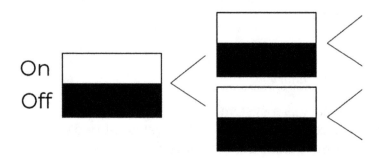

Outside of the computing context, we can establish additional bases for binary in our world of ideas: off/ on, true/false, yes/no, good/bad, or more complicated things like concrete/abstract or happy/sad. These examples partition the world into two parts with seeming opposites.

However, binary choices do not have to focus on *opposite* decisions. For example, if a person gets two job offers, they face a binary choice, although the first job is not the opposite of the second.

Rarely are important decisions in life simple, yet many people subscribe to a binary style of thinking. Sure, it simplifies decision-making, but it costs the entire nuance of existence. We are not robots with simple choices, but skin-covered bags of water and bacteria with outsized brains. If we reduce our thinking to merely good versus bad, we abandon our humanity and shortchange our five senses—not to mention our intellect.

*How is binary useful?*

The world of two gives us the ability to compare. We cannot actually perceive our friend Dottie, for example, without eyeballs *outside* of her with which to observe her. Thus, we cannot describe Dottie without at least one additional Dottie. Dottie is a data point with no contrasting data, and human language only works as a system of references. For example, we cannot claim that Dottie is tall unless we have a shorter Dottie to compare her to. Dottie cannot be the color red unless there exists at least one other color that is not red.

In other words, to say anything interesting about Dottie, we must create a comparison. In order to create comparisons, we must invent differences. As mentioned earlier, comparison is the basis for language. Different-ness is the fundamental basis for our existence. What does it mean to be self-aware? It means seeing ourselves as different from the outside world—the ability to differ-entiate between the inside and the outside. If there is no differentness, then there is no world.

Humans tend to feel their differences acutely. We often feel out of place in nature. Even ancient civiliza-tions grappled with this feeling of disconnection. They told stories describing how man must have first broken from nature. To this day, people wonder whether we can reconcile these differences. Can we reunite with nature? Why do we feel so *other*?

### The birth of the imagination

The birth of the human imagination arises alongside this human break with nature: To have imagination is to feel separate from reality. Let us first examine a human idea that we do not observe in nature: justice. This lack of what we call justice in nature creates the first crack— the cognitive dissonance—that leads us to question our world. In time, this crack becomes a chasm, and just as problems force us to action, our desires for justice lead us to create ethical codes, and eventually to create civi-lization itself.

Whether or not you agree that justice represents the

first irreconcilable difference we have with nature, the problems we encounter as dissatisfied customers lead us inexorably toward imaginative solutions. Armed with an ever-increasing capacity for abstract thought, we invent better and better tools to improve on nature in various ways. Objectivizing nature allows us to question and examine it, to exploit its resources, to copy its patterns for tools. Yet as surely as we feel apart from nature, we are inextricably linked with it.

*More about the human problem of justice*

We live in a fractured world filled with death, disease, hunger, and all manner of physical and psychological pain. We are born unequal in our abilities and means, and societal structures often serve to further these inequalities. Good deeds pass unnoticed or unrewarded, while evil goes unpunished. This problem has been around for thousands of years: "There is something else meaningless that occurs on Earth: righteous men who get what the wicked deserve, and wicked men who get what the righteous deserve." (Ecclesiastes 8:14). What goes around rarely comes around.

Even in our most joyous moments, we are somehow incomplete, perhaps aware of our fading glory or our oncoming death. Whatever the reasons, most of us chuckle along with Arthur Dent from *The Hitchhiker's Guide to the Galaxy* when he says, "I always thought there was something fundamentally wrong with the universe."

We dream about early paradises like the Garden of Eden, Shangri-La, Elysium Fields, and various Golden

Ages from the distant past, where life felt less complicated, things made sense, and peace—or at least good taste—reigned. Most of us recognize these mythical places as nostalgia or fantasy—places that never truly existed. All the same, we fight daily battles with reality. We wish the world would be different, we complain, or at a more self-actualized level, we become the change we wish to see in the world—alas, even the optimists see that something is missing.

Our world is not a paradise—it's not even fair. However, this lack of justice, this seeming imperfection, serves as a major motivator. Lack of justice in the natural world spurs many noble human activities; it certainly sews the seeds for government as an enforcer of social justice. Wherever people live with or near others, justice becomes a major concern. Civilization itself rests upon human ideals of justice, and it will always remain the primary focus of any good government.

In ancient Greece, Socrates and Plato labored to define justice. We benefit from their lack of discovery. Justice is an abstract concept without correspondence to the physical world—a figment of our individual and collective imaginations. Justice exists as an ideal, with stress on the fragment of the word "idea." Plato envisioned a more just society as a meritocracy, where merit lies in intellectual ability—an ability where he, coincidentally, excelled. But is such a system just when we are born on a spectrum of abilities through no fault of our own? Plato's meritocracy is merely a different kind of birthright aristocracy.

Our inner children yearn for us to live in a mechanical Rube Goldberg universe where interesting things happen, one thing leads to another, and in the end, justice prevails. However, since we so often desire justice yet so rarely obtain it, we can reformulate the human problem more generally: our dissatisfaction with the natural world arises because our imaginations differ from reality.

From a more contemporary angle than Plato, social phenomenologist Alfred Schütz hypothesizes that we all live in a shared paramount reality that lacks certain things—in the present case, a closed loop that incorporates justice. The gaps in this paramount reality encourage us to engage in ideation: we attach creative supplemental realities to our shared everyday reality. These supplemental realities incorporate those things that our everyday realities lack. Specifically, supplemental realities contain our ideas about justice, our desire for lack of pain, our wishes for immortality, and everything else we seek but cannot find. Since these supplemental realities exist in the imagination but not the physical world, they require faith—or perhaps a voluntarily shared delusion—which moves them from everyday concerns to the spiritual realm.

*What is duality?*

All these arguments aside, it is only our human perspective on the world that notices anything to be missing. For the birds, the trees, and the bees, the world simply exists. There is nothing to compare it to; it is the paramount—and only—reality. Without human imagination, we would not see this crack in reality between

51

the world as it is and the world as it should be. This problematic chasm between our desires and our reality leads us toward the schizophrenic existence that spiritual teachers call "duality." We find analogies to this dilemma in the physical world—we can proclaim duality at the schisms between mind and body, or the ambiguity standing between our logic and emotion. Neuroscientists might even reason by analogy to the brain: two hemispheres but only one brain.

There are two common pathways out of this dilemma. Either we increase our comfort with ambiguity and dissatisfaction, or we actively pursue integrity—our reintegration into some kind of whole self. The former is the pathway to emotional maturity or adulthood, expressed by writers such as M. Scott Peck. The latter is the spiritual pathway. Either path promises improvement.

*What is integrity?*

In theory, integrity represents the remedy for duality. Integrity means "union" and lies at the endpoint of the integration process. People possess integrity when there are no cracks between their words and their actions, or between their thoughts and their words. We can rely on people who have integrity because their actions are predictable: they do not possess secret motives or agendas. In short, such people are clear and obvious, rather than opaque and complicated.

If integration unites things that are separate, then differentiation disentangles pieces from their larger unity. The baby in the womb undergoes differentiation:

it begins as a simple peanut and slowly becomes something with fingers, toes, arms, legs, and more.

The easiest way to differentiate something is to divide it into two pieces. Duality is the division of one concept, such as "human," into two concepts, such as "mind" and "body." *Anything* can be broken into two partitions; for example, the human world contains two separate and distinct groups: people born in Asia and people not born in Asia. While the universe is one reality, any attempt to describe it necessitates dividing it into two or more pieces.

Just as destruction is easier than creation, differentiation is easier than integration. Science largely concerns itself with differentiation through classification and specification, though that is not its only goal. If we peer into an auto shop and see a car in pieces, it is not enough for us to name each part; we must still put the parts back together to create something useful for transportation. Similarly, science names its little pieces and, with any luck, follows up by usefully recombining them.

Spirituality, on the other hand, focuses on seeing the one made from the many—by integrating various objects and ideas. In fact, spiritual teachings often explicitly state that their goal is to transcend, or overcome, dualistic thinking. Indeed, the topic warrants intense examination because integration, being more difficult than differentiation, also gets significantly less press.

Both differentiation and integration are necessary stages in the learning process, as we will discuss in

Chapter 7. Favoring one direction of the process over the other merely leads to imbalance. As in the case of complex systems where we must examine all the moving parts, we cannot restrict our attention to only one direction of a bidirectional, repeating process.

We will now look at how duality informs our attempts to explain our own origins.

*Three creation stories*

The following creation stories all explain the origin of duality with some striking similarities. Each considers humanity's beginning—and thus our first attempts to grapple with duality. Separated by thousands of years, the first two stories are ancient accounts, while the third is contemporary and biological.

Our first story comes from the Old Testament book of Genesis. True to its name, Genesis begins with its main character creating the world out of the void—dividing night from day, Earth from Heaven, land from sea. In other words, God creates Earth through the process of differentiation—specifically, cutting things into two pieces at a time to create binaries.

Later in the story, Genesis recounts the human "fall from grace" and presages our lifelong struggles to return to an ever-elusive paradise. Specifically, God gives humankind a beautiful garden to live in with only two simple rules: first, do not eat from the Tree of the Knowledge of Good and Evil, and second, do not eat from the Tree of Everlasting Life. (A first-time reader might ask why God places these two trees in the same garden and so close to Adam and Eve in the first place.) Of course, like contrary children, the first order of business for Adam and Eve is to disobey these rules and eat the forbidden fruit. Specifically, they snack on the Tree of Knowledge. God responds by evicting the unruly tenants from Eden before they can eat from the Tree of Life. Upon closer inspection, the reader might realize that, even before eating from the Tree of Knowledge, Adam and Eve must have possessed a preponderance of desire, curiosity, and rascality to make such a temptation possible. Indeed, we wonder if Adam and Eve were perhaps flawed from their very creation.

This story explains how humans fell from grace, but it fails to satisfactorily state *why*. It allows for many possible interpretations. Humans will forsake paradise for curiosity; humans cannot follow even simple rules—as, indeed, the entire history of our species is one of creating rules and then disobeying them. Or we can focus specifically upon humanity's increased knowledge—our self-awareness and newfound shame—as that which foretells our doom.

If Adam and Eve had eaten from both trees, humans would have become gods—for what is God other than an immortal being with vast knowledge? But they only ate from one of the trees, and we have lived in this halfway house ever since—our feet in the clay and our heads in the clouds. Thus, between purely instinctual animal and Godhood, we locate our human condition. It may seem like we are a step above the animals, but our location brings its own problems.

The second creation story comes from Plato's *Symposium*, where Aristophanes tells the partygoers about the origin of love. He recounts how humans originally existed as creatures with four arms and four legs, giving them great speed and strength. Indeed, these creatures were so powerful that the Olympic Gods feared they might climb to Heaven in their quest for power. To prevent such a disaster, Zeus strikes the creatures with lightning bolts, literally cutting them down to size without destroying them altogether. (Perhaps he wants the sacrifices they offer him to keep rolling in.) Zeus cuts these creatures precisely in half—down the center—into the humans we are today, with two arms and two legs. He issues a further threat that, should we become too bold, he shall cut us down again, so that we would have to hop around on one leg.

In the aftermath of this massacre, we humans spend our lives looking for our missing halves. If we find them, we feel love. We wish to meld back into the single creature we were before. Imagine how awkward our lives would be if we were required to search for *three* missing quarters rather than just a single half! As in the Genesis story, humans are left incomplete, in the halfway house toward perfect wholeness—this time more literally.

The third creation story is scientific: We all begin life in two completely separate locations. How can we be in two places at once? I don't know, but it's true. We begin as gametes—an ovum and a sperm—both of which are one-celled. These gametes each carry exactly half our genetic information. They unite in fertilization to form another single-celled organism—and from this time onward, these cells continually divide until a complete human possesses about 37 trillion of them. In addition to this genetic bifurcation, our bodies display a physical division into left and right, and our brains are divided into left and right hemispheres.

These three stories provide reasons why we feel incomplete, fractured—whether we only ate half the fruit, were cut in half by divine will, or are physically borne of two different halves. The first two stories explain that we exist precisely halfway between animals and gods, while the third shows us that we are a bit like two unlike pieces fused together. Even our DNA is a double helix of ordered acid-base pairs.

*How do we use this knowledge?*

"Duality" refers to these imaginary yet consequential notions. Whether in biology or culture, we see many twosomes. What lessons can we draw? First, constructing a binary is simple—perhaps too simple. We can divide anything into two.

Second, it's important to understand duality if we wish to move beyond it. Many spiritual traditions are built upon the premise that we can overcome duality, yet before we can transcend anything, we have to know what we are transcending.

Third, we should not necessarily draw moral conclusions about pairings. Nothing in these stories tells us that two is better than one. In fact, oneness seems to be prized more highly.

*Symmetry*

The idea of binary leads naturally to the concept of symmetry. Throughout much of history, humans have regarded the symmetric as beautiful. We often make our art, tools, and props symmetric. We rate symmetric faces as more attractive. While nature has its own ideas about symmetry, humans possess a shared but different perspective on it. For example, you will not see straight lines and boxes in nature. But it is the hallmark of a human habitat that everything will be straight and boxy: buildings, cars, roads, and coffins.

There are different types of symmetry depending on whether we are discussing math, biology, or something else. Reflection and radial/rotation are the most common. Reflective symmetry is based on the idea of two reflections. Rotational or radial symmetry is not binary but rather symmetry in a circular direction. We are used to reflective symmetry, perhaps due to our experience with mirrors. We rarely think in radial symmetry.

Symmetry is not only visual. Even statistics can present us with symmetry, such as in the normal curve, which we discuss in Chapter 5. The ancient Greeks decided that symmetry was beautiful and therefore truth. Today we follow this habit, but we also have other options to choose from.

Since the aim of this book is to introduce more complex concepts into our thinking, let us now consider the concept of social symmetry. When someone does you a favor, you feel you have a debt of gratitude. One option is to pay that debt forward—in other words, you do a favor for someone new. Another option is to reciprocate. This means doing a different favor for the same person who originally did you a favor. Usually we cannot reciprocate with the exact same favor back;

we just do whatever kind of favor we are capable of. What other ways could we practice social symmetry or reciprocity after receiving a favor?

We can also revolt against symmetry in various ways. There is a Japanese aesthetic called *wabi sabi*. This is the beauty of the dilapidated, lived-in house, the nostalgia in a well-used sofa. The symmetry and newness have been lost to time and entropy. Do you see how this differs from both classical beauty and the pure beauty of nature? We still have straight lines and boxes, but now they are falling apart.

We now conclude with some binary notions that are *not* symmetric, but rather complementary, as in the yin and yang.


*Taoist yin and yang*

The yin-yang is a great example of a natural pattern we can use in our own thinking. This Taoist symbol originates in a natural phenomenon: seasonality. Before the industrial revolution and mass migration to cities, humans were more in touch with nature. Seasonality is an aspect of life that we have lost touch with. Ecclesiastes begins: "To everything there is a season." There is a rhythm to life and to the world. The pendulum swings from day to night, winter to summer, naturally laying the foundation for many early theories.

"Seasonality" refers to a pattern that repeats annually—every time the earth makes one revolution around the sun. Knowledge of seasonality is crucial to agriculture. Indeed, the four seasons of the year are usually the first things that spring to mind at the word "season," but humans also create seasons. We have baseball season, holiday season, tax season, and many others.

The binary schemata of yin and yang dates back to the I Ching (circa 1100 BCE). It began as an observation of nature's seasonal patterns, as shown below. Here we provide the instructions for a do-it-yourself yin-yang.

The shadow of the above pole is marked off each day at the same time, and after one year, the pattern of the markings will resemble the pattern below. Shade one side, add a couple of dots, and you have your own yin-yang.

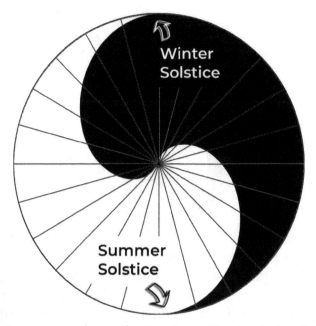

We now see how the Taoist *taijitu* is derived from the annual cycle of the earth's revolution around the sun. It symbolizes the balancing of the female and male aspects, and more generally represents the dialectical nature of opposites, competing yet completing: desire versus acceptance, control versus submission, attachment versus detachment. Extreme fascism and extreme communism—one on the far right of the political spectrum, the other on the far left—appear quite similar in practice.

Now, the ideas of feminine and masculine are not meant to be understood literally. We all possess both aspects. In fact, Jung once implied that the very masculine man is still only about 60 percent masculine.

In brief, Taoism is the philosophy that we should copy the patterns of nature. At the center of mass of the white (yang) side is a black (yin) dot. A three-dimensional representation would show how the yang principle, at its densest point, becomes a speck of the yin, thereby transporting it to the other pole. According to Taoist scholar Alan Watts, "The yin-yang principle is...an explicit duality expressing an implicit unity." In addition to yin constantly becoming yang and vice versa, both yin and yang are in a circle, implying a circular—or seasonal—notion of time.

*How can we use the yin-yang?*

The yin-yang begins much like binary and duality, but then it goes further by showing how opposites interact within a unity. We can use this notion when we examine extreme behaviors. In fact, the yin-yang is the first attempt to describe dialectics, which we will discuss in the next chapter. Dialectics are very useful, though most of us know very little about them.

One final comment about using seasonality in our lives. Distinct from seasonality, cyclicality refers to any pattern that repeats itself over any specified time. While seasons are annual cycles, the cycle of night followed by day is a daily cycle, cicadas live on a thirteen-year cycle, and economic recessions in the United States occur on average every six years. Cycles do not have to begin simultaneously. When we refer to the lifecycle of a human, for example, we observe that people are constantly beginning and ending their roughly seventy-five-year cycles at different times.

Trends, on the other hand, refer to non-repeating patterns that typically increase or decrease over a specified time.

*Key Ideas*

- Binaries are simple to create.

- Binaries are often too simplistic to describe the human social world.

- Binaries are not always opposites.

- Binaries allow us to compare.

- Not all the things we care about can be found in nature.

- Life is not just, but we can try to make it fairer with governments and rules.

- Our ability to imagine different realities sets us apart from most other animals.

- We are in the halfway house of existence.

- Binaries allows us to observe symmetry.

- We can copy nature, or we can try to transcend nature.

- Yin-yang symbolism shows how opposites can be closely related.


*Discussion Questions*

- Can you think of more examples where an extreme behavior suddenly looks like the opposite behavior?

- What are some natural patterns that are neglected in this chapter?

*Suggested Activities*

- Watch: *Groundhog Day*. This movie explores how, given limitless time, a man becomes God-like. If you do not understand why God cast Adam and Eve from Eden to keep them from the Tree of Life, this movie is for you.

- Read: *The Book: On the Taboo Against Knowing Who You Are* by Alan Watts. This book discusses binaries, dualities, and organism-environments with depth and wit.

# chapter
# four

*Dialectics — Arguments — Triunes — Quadrants*

*Overview*

In the last chapter, we looked at ideas related to binary and duality. We observed how binaries present us with two all-or-nothing options, like toggles: yes/no, right/wrong, good/bad. Of course, most of our decisions present more alternatives than this framework accommodates, especially decisions of a social nature. Indeed, seeking wisdom often amounts to seeking out such alternatives.

Historically, political philosopher Jean-Jacques Rousseau coined the term "general will" to describe his belief that a group of reasonable people would eventually reach a consensus. Evidently, Rousseau never participated in a group deciding where to eat dinner, or he would have seen his mistake. Is the person who dislikes pizza simply wrong on the merits? Notwithstanding that few people are truly *reasonable,* our unique histories, tastes, and experiences assure that true consensus will rarely occur. Two people reaching agreement on anything is a cause for celebration. Three or more and it's a miracle.

In this chapter, we first explore how two opposing ideas can seem correct at the same time. Then we examine what happens when two different viewpoints clash and lead to arguments, compromises, or new ideas. We end the chapter by looking at how triunes and quadrants can help us structure our thinking.

*What is a dialectic?*

The word "dialectic" has several meanings. In ancient Greece, Socrates used a dialectical method to teach. He discussed ideas with another person, and the two agreed to remove their emotions from the situation in an attempt to create the best rational answer to a question. In reality, Socrates mostly posed questions and poked holes in his partner's answers. This is quite fascinating, especially the first time you read one of these dialogues.

Dialectics is a method used to discover the truth when given two opposing viewpoints. Resolutions of a dialectic come in various forms: the validation of one viewpoint over the other, the discovery of a middle ground, or the transcendence of the dialectic.

In the present day, psychologists often follow a similar route by pointing out our cognitive biases and the statistical errors we make on a daily basis. It is often more difficult to tell someone *how to think* than it is to tell them all the ways they are wrong. Just as destruction is easier than creation, this seems to be an asymmetric law of nature. Constructing a building takes years; destroying it takes seconds. Similarly, in the context of morality, we almost intuitively know what *not* to do, yet we often struggle with what positive actions to take. Expanded morality, more quantified by the new school of effective altruism, is a recent movement in this positive direction.

A second meaning of "dialectic" is extremely useful yet almost unknown in America. Remember back in Chapter 1, where we discussed how our evolutionary heritage pulls us in multiple directions at once. Well, most of us possess an imaginary ideal in our heads that we try to live up to—the norms or standards of some idealized person that we should be. This second definition of dialectic counters the illusion of ideal traits. It shows how we often stumble upon two quite opposing needs—both of which we want—with neither extreme particularly better than the other. The perfect example for this is our simultaneous desires for both independence and human connection. Good luck finding a person who doesn't want a bit of both of these opposed desires.

Psychologist Erik Erikson created a list of these dialectical challenges. His framework included stages we must navigate as we age from young to old. In his model, each stage presents an internal psychological battle we must solve before we can advance to the next stage. For example, early on we are faced with trust or mistrust of the world. Erikson claims that healthy people choose trust, which is kind of a leap. Rather, I think we choose which people and things to trust and mistrust. Remember that models are simplifications of reality, and in the real world, most of these dialectical battles are not winnable.

More examples of these dialectics are found in Jung's archetypes or the Myers-Briggs personality framework. We can choose feeling or we can choose thinking. This dichotomy is merging into one idea lately: our emotions and cognition are not as separate as classical distinction would lead us to believe. In fact, one of the hallmarks of wisdom is an integration or culling of the information contained in *both* feeling and thinking.

Another important dialectic is between subject and object. We are subjects that possess agency to follow our destiny, yet we are simply objects to everyone else. In fact, institutional, educational, and cultural values determine most of our desires. Thus, both ideas of subject and object—agent and puppet—are true at the same time. We might therefore ask which idea is most *useful* for us to believe. In Chapters 6 and 7, we will delve more deeply into how the distinction between subjects and objects can guide our thinking.

How can we solve impossible dialectics? Well, for many of us, we simply swing like a pendulum back and forth between our two opposing needs. We spend a little time here, then a little time there. For example, when we live in isolation, we can simply imagine or remember the times when we were connected—and vice versa.

*The upshot of dialectics*

Now, why is this important? Imagine our discussion in the context of goal-setting. The underlying idea of dialectics is that both poles represent worthwhile aims, so neither one is the ultimate answer. Similarly, when we set our own goals, we can bet that some of them are incompatible. We cannot usually pursue a music career *and also* become a corporate president.

Importantly, the very act of deciding upon something causes us to experience an interesting psychological change. When we choose to follow a certain path, we begin to value it more. *The Little Prince* is a short and wise book that illustrates this phenomenon.

Two important examples of our power to direct our destinies come from *The Little Prince* in the contexts of taming an animal and falling in love. The book's narrator introduces us to a fox and a rose. He tames the fox using the incremental approach: slowly inching toward it, a little closer every day. The attention means that this particular fox becomes different from all the rest. Hence, an enemy gradually becomes a friend. Similarly, the rose he waters becomes special to him—different from all the other roses in the garden. It is our own attention to something that gives the relationship meaning.

Let us imagine a rose garden. All the roses are beautiful. How can we be expected to pick a favorite? Yet this is what we must do if we are to become intimate: we must choose a rose and assure it that it is the best rose of them all. Now a funny thing happens within our psyche. Since we have enacted our choice, we begin to place greater value upon our decision. We weren't fooling anyone, this was definitely the best rose all along! It was clear from the start! In other words, not only do we value something more *because we have chosen it*, we rewrite history to erase the idea that our opinion changed in the first place.

There are downsides to these phenomena. A friend is a wonderful thing—until that friend dies. But "the pain then is part of the pleasure now," as Joy tells C. S. Lewis in the movie *Shadowlands*. The unnoticed transformation of opinion is also a problem because no one admits to changing. We do not like the existential insecurity it implies. Furthermore, once we have completed a decision, that decision often becomes a part of our identity. In general, it is wiser to subtract things from our identity than add them, which we will discuss more deeply in Chapter 7. For now, suffice it to say that we must discover the joy of being wrong—in arguments, in life, in love.

In sum, we create our own meaning, and we often do it after the fact. For this reason, we should not avoid making decisions. "Not making a decision" is still a kind of decision—we cannot escape the circle of life. Thus, we should listen when motivational author Louise Hay advises us to *be decisive*. If you make a wrong decision, make another decision.

### Freud's dialectics

While Aristotle speaks in terms of the good life, Freud calls out the flawed life. They are looking at the problem from opposite directions. While Aristotle advises us to seek moderation in all things, Freud warns us that deviance from the norm causes suffering. Freud thus implies that mature adults are mature because they lack neuroses, not because they have mastered any particular positive attributes. Only since the 1990s has positive psychology focused on enhancing positive traits rather than merely minimizing negative ones. We have slowly returned to Aristotle's old ideas on how to live a fulfilled life through self-examination—the remediation of under-developed skills, but more importantly the development of positive attributes.

Freud's main contribution to theory is his recognition that our own minds are of two parts—yet another dialectic. In this case, the schism is between the conscious mind and the subconscious mind. This knowledge is now so ingrained in our culture that it's difficult to comprehend how people studied behavior before this realization.

While the conscious mind is the seat of the ego, Freud further divides the subconscious mind into two parts: the superego and the id. A tension exists between these two opposing parts, as they represent our most-evolved and least-evolved aspects: our morals and our animal natures. In this framework, it is not other people we are at war with—it is ourselves. Indeed, perhaps we wage wars with other people precisely *because* we are at war with ourselves.

Freud performed two bifurcations in turn: subconscious and conscious, then id and superego. He leaves us with three constraints to our behavior—a trialectic. We are constrained in our decision-making by the ego, which acts as our sense of self; the superego, which acts as our moral compass; and the id, which is our animal relic—the so-called reptilian brain with its fight-or-flight responses.

*How can we be more mindful in disagreements?*

How do we approach people with different viewpoints than our own? We usually choose from a few options: argument, debate, and conversation. An argument begins as a reaction, usually emotional, based on differences of opinion. The intention is usually to restore one's egoic feeling of being whole or in the right. A debate, however, is quite different. It is a format with less emotional commitment, where neither party actually expects to change their own minds. Debaters use emotional appeals to their audiences, but they do not usually experience emotions themselves. Finally, a conversation is agreed upon beforehand, contains emotional information, and is open-ended with regard to any intended outcome. That is, we do not enter a conversation with the intention of proving the other person wrong, but perhaps we may change our own minds. As we discussed in Chapter 1, a conversation is where both parties listen with open minds, creating a cooperative improvisational dance of language and meaning without a predetermined outcome. We enter conversations to change *and* be changed.

Most of our interactions are more simply termed "discussions": exchanges of information during which we engage in small talk or recount our latest activities. The terminology here is not the point; rather, what assumptions can we question from these explanations? For example, do arguments happen *to* us, or do we approach them intentionally? Should a debater simply try to win at all costs? Are foregone conclusions a fair way to approach real disagreements? Can we make conversations a more favored approach over arguing and debating? How do we signal our intentions to another person? (We will discuss this last question in great detail in Chapter 8.)

If there were only two people left on Earth, they would surely find something to argue about. Like dogs who mark their territories, we would argue about land or some other resource, be it scarce or abundant. So how do we best approach disagreements with other people? Ideally, assuming we are open-minded sorts, we first give the other person the validation discussed in Chapter 1. Second, we radically listen to their viewpoints. Third, we define our terms. Perhaps the other person is simply pulling their words from a different dictionary, but we need a shared glossary to have a fruitful conversation. Fourth, we provide the other person with our "new" information. Perhaps they simply do not know all the facts that we are privy to. In other words, we approach our disagreement as a fact-finding mission. Finally, when we have these points out of the way, we can begin with emotion. Emotion is not *worse* than reason. We typically attempt reason before emotions, but you can try it the other way around—just keep in mind that you are battling tradition.

Even though this all sounds quite idealized, we could begin the entire sequence with even *more* awareness on our parts. For example, what is the ultimate goal in this exchange? Do we even need to engage with this person at all? Is this the correct person to engage with? Do we simply seek validation of our common humanity? Do we want the other person to just hear our information? Do we want to actually change this person's viewpoint? In short, what is our *intention* for engaging in conversation with this person? These questions all lead to very different events.

Intention is always very important—again, not because it helps anyone else, but because it forces us to be honest with ourselves. We gain inner clarity when we know the reasons we do what we do. If we can pinpoint the outcome we desire, we can move toward that outcome more deliberately.

Obviously, opinions are tricky things. We never know why people hold them. Some people simply love to argue or debate and do not seek conciliation. Some would rather win or lose than compromise. Are our ego identities at risk here? Will even new information fail to move someone? When we examine why people hold certain beliefs, we may find it has nothing at all to do with information. For example, people often honor their parents by attending the same church their parents did. Very few people shop for churches. Would the discovery of new facts about religion or new revelatory information change behavior of this sort?

What other paths might we pursue in a civil argument? In addition to sharing new information and marking out emotional or other boundaries, an argument might focus on pointing out some common mistakes in thinking. While some of these are simply variations on a theme, there are hundreds of well-researched cognitive biases. They tend to be systematic logical fallacies or errors in statistical thinking.

We do not all suffer from every bias. However, very few of us take classes in logic or statistics. Thus, we can find plenty of personal biases to correct. Many other books look at these biases, so I will not detail them here, but I'll provide a few related ideas in Chapter 10.

What are the possible outcomes for a debate or argument made in good faith—meaning that both parties are willing to change their opinions? The potential outcomes have two main variations: both parties could stand pat, or one or both could change their view. If either party alters their stance at all, the world has shifted a bit. We do not have to leave an encounter with full agreement for meaningful change. Recall from Chapter 2 that pursuing incremental change is enough.

*What are triunes?*

We now turn now to the concept of "triune"— something with three parts. Here we look again at the Golden Rule. We examine a framework where the Golden Rule—"do unto others as you would have them to do unto you"— implies three different cases. In the Preface, I mentioned that we could collapse this advice into a unity: that how you treat others is how you treat yourself. In this case, there is no advice; there is only an observation. Now imagine: we treat others worse than we treat ourselves, we treat others better than we treat ourselves, we treat others the same as we treat ourselves. Respectively, we call these three parts a "superiority complex," an "inferiority complex," and no complex. Thus, we have three cases.

What general principles can we derive from this

triune? Most importantly, we can see how superiority complexes are similar to inferiority complexes. They are now part of the same conceptual model, where perhaps before we did not understand how they were related. Additionally, we can now see that both are struggles against reality. If we are equal to one another, inferiority and superiority complexes are called "complexes" precisely because they are mistakes. What they share in this example: they are both mistakes of not realizing one's equality to others.

We now examine a more common triune. In position papers, or essays that we write for school, we often use a format called "thesis, antithesis, and synthesis." This is the written method to resolve arguments. The original thesis, or opinion, is laid out. The antithesis is the opposing viewpoint. Thus, we could posit that humans are animals. The counterargument is that humans are not animals—they are different. The paper would then give evidence and arguments on both sides of the issue. The final synthesis shows a more sophisticated restatement of the original thesis. For example, the new opinion is that humans are *unique* animals. The synthesis is a compromise of sorts, but a compromise that is more powerful in some sense than the original statement because it contains more nuance. (We will resume this point in Chapter 6.)

Of course, the most famous triad is the Trinity— the Father, Son, and Holy Ghost—all three different and yet all one at the same time. We might imagine this concept as a triangle. A triangle is a strong shape; we often use it for a tripod's legs, so it doesn't wobble.

Often, we think two words or concepts are opposites, but a closer look reveals *three* connected ideas. For example, in a famous song from the Broadway musical *Rent*, the cast sings: "The opposite of war isn't peace... it's creation!" If you have not heard this before, take a moment to let the meaning sink in. If we envision war as destruction, then the opposite action is not mere peace, as we usually assume. In fact, the opposite of destruction *is* creation. We construct a building, we demolish a building, or we leave it alone. If we envision a line with creation and destruction at the two poles, we would place "peace" somewhere in the middle.

*destruction – peace – creation*

Likewise, theorist Nassim Taleb explains how "fragile" and "robust" can be understood in a way that is different from mere opposites. The opposite of something fragile is not something strong, but rather something that gains from experiencing headwinds. The opposite of fragile is *anti-fragile*. An anti-fragile system gains from a storm where the fragile system collapses. Indeed, this is why we should adopt flexible thinking: rigid structures are the first to collapse in a storm. When we are flexible thinkers, we are more adaptable to new circumstances.

People cannot be opposites. People are much more complicated than that—even if we could find the two most extreme exemplars. We all simply have too much in common to be opposites.

79

Finding opposites is a tricky process, and context matters. If asked for the opposite of "slow," most of us would say "fast." But consider this graphic:

<< *fast* << *slow* << *stopped* >> *slow* >> *fast*

Robert Sternberg, one of the earliest contemporary researchers to theorize about wisdom, often uses a triadic form which he calls triarchic. He is most famous for his triarchic theory of intelligence to replace the notion of single metrics like the intelligence quotient. Freud also used the triadic form. But it remains unpopular.

*Fours and quadrants*

The idea of *four* is quite popular in both science and social science. When we place two different binaries or continuums together into one diagram with horizontal and vertical axes, we get the following shape:

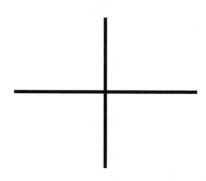

Where before we had two separate binary distinctions, we now have four different interactions. The binaries must relate in some way for this to make any sense. One common binary is good versus bad. When we combine this with the binary of happy versus sad, here is what we get:

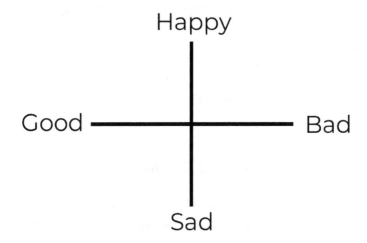

What does this graph show us? In the upper right quadrant, we have an observation that something is happy yet bad. We could call this bittersweet. Likewise, the lower left quadrant is good yet sad. This is some form of nostalgia. But this graph does not say anything very useful or interesting. However, when we add certain binaries together, we get a much deeper tunderstanding of an issue. The movement from two concepts to four could be called "nuance." The more nuances we have in our understanding, the more sophisticated—or expert—our understanding.

Let us look at the idea of accuracy versus precision.

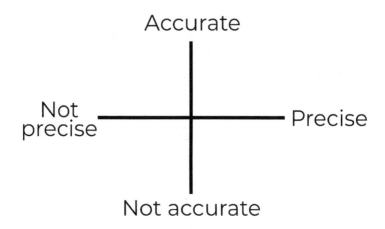

First, we define what "accuracy" and "precision" mean. "Accuracy" is how closely an idea resembles some sort of objective truth. "Precision," on the other hand, is how closely repeated measurements of a thing will agree with one another. If your measuring tool is skewed strongly to the left, for example, it can be very precise without being accurate. If your measuring tool is very poor, it can be neither precise nor accurate. If the measuring device is more like buckshot but always seems to give useful results, we could say it is accurate but not precise.

In politics, a more sophisticated approach than simply calling ideology left or right is to combine two axes—one for the economic left and right, the second for libertarian versus authoritarian. Instead of two different groups of people, we now have four. Similarly, from the Myers-Briggs personality test we have four different binaries that yield sixteen different personality types.

Obviously we don't want to use one hundred different personality types, because the model becomes too complex for us to understand. This is called the "parsimony versus explanatory problem," which is yet another binary-like continuum. Almost anything we say about other people is a generalization. We don't want to stereotype people, but our minds must succumb to a certain level of prejudging or we would become too insecure to get out of bed in the morning.

You could try an experiment for a day in which you make no assumptions about anything. That is how a true mystic lives. For most of us, the best we can do is to try to keep our stereotypes for deeper considerations than race, appearance, gender, etc. As in everything, awareness is half the battle. Ultimately, we then try to make our mental models as nuanced as we can each personally handle.

In the next chapter, we add a new twist to the idea of binary: how to describe the *quantity* of people that fit along the various points of a continuum. That is, we will examine how various traits are distributed among a population. In Chapter 6 we will extend our discussion of triads in the form of thesis, antithesis, and synthesis into the shape of a helix.

*Key Ideas*

- A dialectic is a discussion or movement between two opposing ideas.

- A dialectic can result in one option over the other, a compromise, or some kind of transcendence.

- Destruction is easier than creation.

- Expanded morality is the most good we can do, rather than the least harm.

- The mere act of deciding changes the value we place upon our choice.

- Not deciding is still a type of deciding.

- There are important differences between arguments, debates, and conversations.

- We can choose how to act and react with arguments.

- Triunes have three parts—for example: thesis, antithesis, and synthesis.

- We must be careful about what we consider to be opposites.

- We can add two binary notions together to form four quadrants for greater nuance.

*Discussion Questions*

- What are some dialectics you have dealt with? Did you ever transcend a dialectic, or did you simply lose interest?

- What are some additional examples of triunes or mistaken opposites?

- What are some possible ways to do the most good rather than merely avoiding doing bad?

- What are some interesting ways to combine binaries in quadrants? Can you imagine more than two binaries in a single graph?

- What are some considerations regarding stereotyping versus living without any assumptions

# chapter five

## Norm - Norms - The Normal Curve - Social Science

*Overview*

When we pursue wisdom, we dance to the offbeat. The path to spiritual independence does not normally conform to convention, however wisdom does include knowing what makes the typical person tick—even though we climb our own ladders.

In the last chapter, we looked at how we might approach arguments with a single other person, how two equally salient ideals might mean that our behavior oscillates between two very different endpoints, and how binary distinctions might often be triunes in disguise. In this chapter, we will increase the complexity of these ideas by examining the concept of binary in a more sophisticated and contemporary way. Specifically, this chapter examines Norm, a fictitious person whom we measure ourselves against. Then we define and analyze some more general types of norms. Next we examine the normal curve used in statistical thinking. We end by discussing some differences between science and social science.

## The Normal Curve

While I sound some alarm bells here about using the normal curve, many of our cognitive biases are tied to a poor understanding of statistics—or the illusion that they only apply to other people. I recommend learning statistics in order to think more effectively. The normal curve originally showed how frequently we encounter various measurement errors. It was only later that people mistakenly began to think of an average measurement as an *ideal* measurement. In fact, the man who coined the term "normal curve," biostatistician Karl Pearson, even remarked that data does not *normally* follow this distribution.

However, for one hundred years, the normal curve's popularity has only increased—encroaching ever more deeply into our worldviews. The over-quantification of the world remains a human threat, whether lost in numbers when strategizing about mass genocide or simply losing sight of the bigger picture of life during very specialized research. Since we live inside a universal open system and are ourselves reflective, we can never collapse the world into one equation. As Alan Watts would say, this would be like biting our own teeth. A tool cannot tool itself.

*Who is Norm?*

Norm is the typical person and does not exist—as no one is average in every domain. (Interestingly, we do rate average faces as more attractive.) As a path to wisdom, the idea that we should strive for moderation is found in Aristotle's Golden Mean. In my own experience, however, the truth is rarely moderate—it is whatever it is. Let's go ahead and meet Norm. He is waving hello. Norm is the mascot for this chapter.

First off, if Norm is from the United States, he is roughly 52% female. But Norma is busy working in a different book, so we've booked Norm. Norm likes to color inside the lines—even while thinking outside the box. Norm is like an Average Joe or Plain Jane. He or she conforms to the plain or the average.

Norm is famous yet misunderstood. Everybody knows Norm, but not everyone likes him. He is certainly a well-meaning chap, if not quite up to date on all the latest trends. He lives in an average-sized house, drives an average car, and has 1.9 children. His parents, with 87% likelihood, were born in the United States. He believes in God *and* evolution. Typically, Norm wants more sleep and more money.

What are your impressions of Norm? Do you aspire to be Norm—to be like him? Asked differently, would you prefer to be an average thinker or an exceptional thinker? Statistically, the average thinker tbelieves he or she is above average. In fact, the overconfidence bias suggests that we *all* feel a bit better than Norm—which of course is impossible for more than half of us. Many of us are, by definition, *worse* than Norm in any given domain. So if most of us don't aspire to be Norm, why do we pay him so much attention?

In the United States, we live in an aspirational culture. What do we aspire to? While we may no longer compete with the Joneses in buying newer kitchen appliances, we still seek self-improvement— and like other primates, we will always seek a higher rung in the social hierarchy. Unfortunately, we are not overly creative in defining what this hierarchy actually measures. We rightly torpedoed the British idea of a birthright aristocracy, but we left a hierarchy vacuum that only money has filled.

Consider the case of Finland, where teachers are highly respected. In the United States, on the other hand, respect for professions correlates to pay, and teachers are not paid well. Taken to its extreme, we laud greedy and unscrupulous moneychangers over hardworking and honest laborers. But is not higher pay reward enough for people? Why should certain people benefit twice, by earning money *and* respect? As a culture, could we begin competing more along dimensions of wisdom, empathy, and altruism? Or could we simply compete against our former selves—as mentioned in Chapter 1—and pursue self-improvement?

Philosopher Rudolf Steiner says, "We no longer believe that there is a norm to which we must all strive to conform." In his younger years, my father felt that he was "normal" and that many other people were not. Now that he is 91, he says he is an old man rather than a normal person. From years of interacting with my father, I have rebelled against this notion, and now my bias is against the very use of the word "normal." I do not possess a standard of normality. People are unique, diverse—and welcome in my ingroup. We'll talk more about ingroups in Chapter 7.

A slightly different perspective on this attitude is offered by philosopher and logician Bertrand Russell: "Conventional people are roused to fury by departures from convention, largely because they regard such departures as a criticism of themselves." From this perspective, we see how a fragile ego might cling to the ideas of norms. To me—and perhaps Bertrand—a person who calls others abnormal, or not normal, often signals that this person will soon say something bigoted.

*What else does the word "norm" mean?*

In addition to the ideas of average and ideal people, the word "norm" can refer to other concepts. There are different types of norms, such as social norms, cultural norms, and actual statistics. Norms are often simply standards or models of behavior. By following norms, someone exhibits acceptable behavior within a group's set of principles. The second meaning of "norms"— according to Merriam-Webster—are those principles of behavior that we would call highly ethical. There is yet a third definition that simply implies average or typical behavior.

What are we to conclude from these three quite different meanings? Are norms merely value-free models of behavior, are they exemplars of high virtue, or are they simply the default average? No wonder we face a quandary about how to behave.

When we join new groups, we learn the expected norms and consciously or subconsciously imitate these standards—especially when we are trying to belong. If we are an outsider to a group, however, we might complain that a group's morality is not high enough, not strict enough, or some other complaint. Some ethical people let their morals slip when they're constantly exposed to corner-cutters, which is called the "normalization of deviance." Does this mean, conversely, that bad people can be saved by hanging out with people who exhibit prosocial behavior? Novelist Victor Hugo certainly thought so when he wrote *Les Misérables*. In that book, Jean Valjean is saved by a bishop who shows him what mercy means, and Valjean follows a path of high morals ever after. The bishop quotes to Valjean from the book of Luke: "There will be more rejoicing in Heaven over one sinner who repents than over ninety-nine righteous persons who do not need to repent." (Luke 15:7)

Traditionally, however, when we study ethics, we are told what *not* to do—who not to kill in the trolley problem. If we want to do the most good, however, we have to be more creative. There is endless suffering in the world, and we all have finite time. But there is plenty of room to do *more* good. Recently, the concept of "effective altruism" has emerged, urging us to tithe toward charity in a more systematic fashion. We can financially analyze the charities we support to reward the highest good. If we do not have money to give, our most precious resource is always time. If we have neither money nor time, we can use our everyday encounters to promote goodwill. Express gratitude, respect people, forgive others, hand someone this book—the list goes on.

*The normal curve: binaries versus spectra*

We see that Norm is an elusive person—an illusion. In fact, Norm is not a person at all, but a mathematical idea. Statisticians depict Norm graphically, which allows us to easily observe the average and distribution of certain phenomena. In other words, Norm does not really exist in nature, but we use him to explain natural phenomena.

We studied binaries to such an extent in the last few chapters partly because we needed to lay the groundwork to fully understand Norm. You see, Norm grows out of binary thinking. That does not make him bad, but you should already be thinking about how this might limit him. The right and left sides of Norm are called "tails." These represent the extremes of the particular issue under examination. A normal curve generally studies one issue at a time. If you are remembering Aristotle's Golden Mean right now, kudos to you. In many ways, the normal curve is a graphical depiction of the Golden Mean.

Like the yin-yang symbol, we often divide the world into two complete and opposing sections. For example, half of the earth is the Northern Hemisphere, and the other half is the Southern Hemisphere. We illustrate—and mentally imagine—this idea by picturing a globe. In this case, both parts are equal, opposite, and without any overlap.

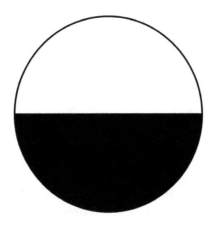

As we saw in Chapter 3, humans add the two balancing black and white dots to the centers of the opposing sides of the yin-yang. These dots are not part of the natural shadow but artifacts of human thinking. Human concepts and ideas often have a funny way of going in circles—a bit like the effects that mirrors create when they face one another—bending our reflections a million times. In fact, without using clear landmarks, such as choosing certain trees in a forest, we even end up *walking* in circles.

Can we use the yin-yang symbol to visualize binary distinctions where 25 percent of the world is one way and 75 percent is the opposing way? What if there are overlapping parts? What if the parts are not really opposites? In these cases, we need something more complicated than the yin-yang.

We now pull out last chapter's triunes: the horizontal model with its three points. We stretch it upward to show the popularity of various points along the line— the higher this line, the more occurrences we observe. It is just common convention to stretch the lines upward; we could stretch them in any direction.

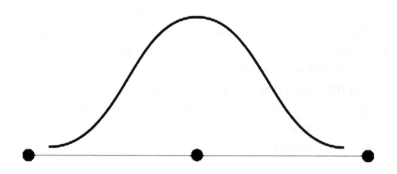

Nature often creates spectra rather than binaries, but this sort of complexity is a lot more difficult to think about. We've previously discussed simple black-and-white thinking. When the world is more complex than this, we use a spectrum or continuum. A spectrum is simply a line with two endpoints, where observations of a thing fall anywhere along the line. We know that binary thinking is easy for our brains to handle. Spectrum thinking is much more complex because spectra come in a wider variety of mathematical types.

We will now briefly examine three types of spectra: discrete, bumpy, and the normal distribution. A distribution tells us how popular any location on the spectrum is.

"Discrete" means that the categories exist only as whole numbers or values. If we are counting how many children a group of people have, the options are thus discrete.

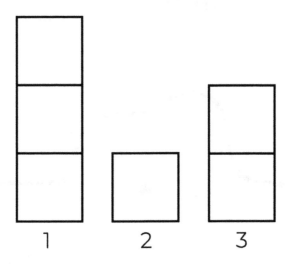

1      2      3

The alternative to discrete is "continuous," or what we call a spectrum. If we are measuring anything that can take on a range of values, including fractions, we use a graph where the upper line is curved but continuous: a bumpy distribution.

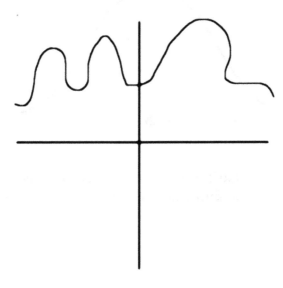

Finally, the normal curve looks like this:

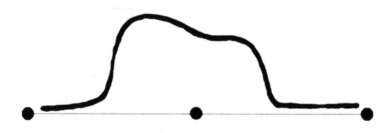

I don't know how that got in here—someone's idea of a joke. Here is the actual normal-curve distribution:

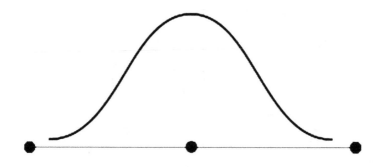

Scientists like the normal curve because it is symmetric and they can find values like the average at a glance.

*What are some problems with the normal curve?*

The main problem with the normal curve is that nature creates infinite variety, while society creates norms. In a not-always-subtle way, diversity is flattened to a single idea or norm. Instead of a spectrum of values and paths, we are shunted through school, through social institutions, and through corporate life. At worst, creativity is actively discouraged. But the imagination is the main human gift to the universe.

Norm and the normal curve like to hide information. Imagine a car with two drivers who behave very differently. One recklessly speeds everywhere, the other goes extremely slow. Looking from a distance, we cannot see who is driving. The drivers swap places when the car is in a closed garage. We thus think there is only one driver. When all the car's speeds are averaged out, the car's average speed is simply average! See how the normal curve hides a two-headed monster?

Let me cite a better example. After I watched the movie *Cloud Atlas*, I rushed to read the reviews. I loved the movie, but it required understanding six different stories at the same time, as well as enjoying six different genres. The meta-critic score was exactly average at 50. What was missing in this single statistic, however, was the way the ratings were distributed. Upon reading actual reviews, I found that half the reviewers loved the movie and the other half hated it. But what a score of 50 is usually assumed to mean is that nearly every reviewer found the movie mediocre—a completely different sentiment than we have here.

Speaking of conforming to norms, we also encounter

the popularity trade-off. For example, how much art is a movie like *Cloud Atlas* prepared to sacrifice for higher ticket sales? In a market with commodity pricing, the movies and art that are most popular will be the most successful. Popularity may work well for politics, but it becomes a strange goal to aim for in music, literature, or any other art.

*How is social science different from science?*

This book is neither social science nor science. But what characterizes or defines these categories? Science and social science are both ways of understanding the world, both performed by human researchers, and both based on presenting certain evidence. Both get plenty of things wrong. Some scientists mistakenly think science gets the last word, but philosophy gets the first and last word on everything. I do not mean the academic discipline of philosophy here, but rather the human philosophy of the heart and mind—our personal motivations, ideas, and limitations. These are our world's most important questions, but they are only studied by a hearty handful of independents, psychologists, and philosophers. That said, social science and science are very useful tools. They may not be steering the ship, but they are rowing furiously. If they do get occasional chances to steer, it is only because a human somewhere allowed it. Someone planted inside both fields or outside altogether is required to explain how the two differ.

Why are these distinctions important? Knowledge empowers us. We call this power our "spirit" or "will."

In science, we possess the freedom to choose what to study. Through knowledge, we learn to prevent and cure diseases. Meanwhile, in social science, we learn how to improve institutions or ourselves. For example, by learning common cognitive biases, we can eventually—in the long run—overcome these biases through education and institutional change. Indeed, human flourishing is the aim of wisdom.

First, the half-lives—or lifespans—of the findings are much shorter in social science. Social science relies more heavily on context. Humans are not as easy to predictably manipulate as atoms or molecules—or anything else scientists study. When the social world changes, new tests can get new results.

Second, the social sciences use averages. At least until quantum uncertainty, science did not rely on averages. Imagine a scientist claiming that the average helium atom has a certain property. This is simply not how scientists speak. All helium atoms are exactly identical and will predictably repeat their past behavior.

Third, social science theories differ from physical and biological theories because they always contain elements of reflexivity. Philanthropist George Soros adapts this idea of reflexivity from philosopher Karl Popper to explain that, because humans reflect and learn, we can never become the static objects of experiments. We can change our actions based on new information, especially when this new information relates to a theory under question. When we change our actions, the experiment leads to a different result. We can even be primed subliminally to change our actions without our overt knowledge. With time, we can even change

101

our subconscious beliefs, so reflexivity is here to stay. Said differently, since we participate in life, we cannot simultaneously observe it. When we try to become a non-participant observer, as early anthropologists attempted, we are either faced with a very limited understanding of what we observe, or—as anthropology might argue today—we are misguided from the outset to seek some kind of privileged observer status. Our results will be neither true nor ethical. Of course, if we value consciousness as the most important aspect of things, this bias can later turn against us when extraterrestrials visit or dolphins suddenly evolve.

*Parting thoughts: norms, rules, and models of behavior*

In the Old Testament, Moses presents a new set of rules. We start with ten of them, literally written in stone, which should make them very clear and impressive. However, if we examine just one of them, "Thou shalt not kill," we can already see problems arising in the periphery, especially if we have read *Animal Farm* or examined a law book. The minute a law is written, the impulse is to test it, curious creatures that we are. Indeed, most people today interpret this law idiosyncratically. Most of us accept the killing of plants and animals. Many of us accept killing in wartime, in self-defense, in euthanasia, as governmental punishment for murder, and many other exceptions.

Instead of language, we can try using a model. A model is the visual representation of one or more theories. We do not look to them for truth; rather they provide useful predictions or explanations through metaphor. We observe three general trends arching over models of behavior.

First, we see a movement toward greater complexity—specifically, more variables and constraints fall under consideration. While the forms gradually become more sophisticated, the deep and unsolvable puzzles of existence remain even in the most primitive frameworks. Advances in mathematics and computing power have enabled and propelled an increase in sophistication, but science does not contain its own motive. It is only philosophy that tells us which questions to pursue within science.

Second, while the early models tend to be prescriptive—advising people how to behave—the later models are positive, explaining *how* people behave. This evolution is in part deliberate, as social science takes its cues from natural science. It also results from psychology's relatively recent focus on motivations and the subconscious as the driving factors in behavior, with the idea that perhaps we should fully understand these invisible forces before attempting to change them.

Third, the models gradually move from general rules of behavior to specific instances. In legal terms, such a movement appears as the gradual evolution from equity to code law. In the United States, we currently live under both systems, but because code law is self-propagating, codes increase exponentially, while equity refers to an abstract notion that can be referenced using a single word: fairness. Instead of following Ten Commandments, we now follow thousands of rules—most of which we cannot even enumerate. While this move from the general to the specific parallels the aforementioned increase in sophistication, it remains a distinct phenomenon: the study of general behavior gives way to the study of granular decision-making in particular contexts. Although it may seem counterintuitive, the advent of more rules does not stifle the spirit. Indeed, depending upon cultural settings and contexts, there is good evidence that rules can create freedom.

In conclusion, we are most blind to ourselves, as the Johari window illustrates. In this vein, psychology, like economics, can never be anything other than a social science because it is reflexive. Subjects can change their behaviors when they receive new information—especially theoretical information about how they should behave. However, this is precisely what makes psychology and other social sciences so interesting.

*Key Ideas*

- Wisdom is not conformist.

- Norm does not exist.

- We should be careful about what standards we choose to follow.

- People are unique and diverse.

- Doing the least harm is different from doing the most good.

- The normal curve is popular but has some issues when it becomes a standard.

- The normal curve hides information.

- As their different names suggests, social science differs from physical or biological science.

- We get a lot of advice about how we should not behave, but less about how we *should* behave.

*Discussion Questions*

- What are some examples of times when the average of something is neither true nor useful?

- What are some additional ways that social science differs from natural science?

- What are some rules of behavior that tell us how to behave, rather than what not to do?

# chapter six

## Felix the Helix

*Overview*

We have looked at binary, triunes, dialectics, and norms. We now illustrate how to mark progress in our thinking. In this chapter, we will look at how to transcend some apparent opposites. Then we will update some of the ideas about spiritual maturity that psychiatrist and author M. Scott Peck discussed in his first book, *The Road Less Traveled*, which has sold over 7 million copies. Finally, we look at causal loops and spiral causation—things like avalanches and snowball effects.

Let's begin by examining the visual pattern that results when we overcome or transcend apparent opposites.

*How do we transcend opposites?*

Not every binary distinction of opposites is recon-cilable—but some are, especially in theory and knowl-edge. We already discussed how the person who feels better than everyone is *similar* to the person who feels worse than everyone. Now let's look at this idea graph-ically. The opposites are transcended in the realization that we are *equal* to other people. We can show this as a triangle where the new, higher level of consciousness is above and between the two old levels.

We now sit at this higher level. However, we still live in a binary or dialectical world. Until we reach full enlightenment—or death—we will always have pieces we need to further integrate or fight. Thus, the third dot above becomes part of a new system: we add another dot at the same level and must then climb to the top of the triangle yet again. When we graph a second instance of overcoming a new dialectical quandary, we obtain five points, as shown below. Our path is like an upward zigzag.

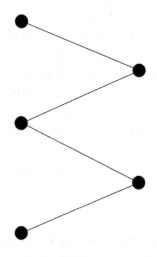

In certain cases, the dots on the right side will have something in common, and the dots on the left side will share a common factor. If we picture a succession of these realizations, we eventually draw a helix or spiral.

Helix

Now, it's difficult to give concrete examples of this. It is often clearest with the same example of introversion versus extroversion that we used before. You can find additional examples on the internet. Here, we can picture the right dots as relating to "independence" and the left dots as "connection with other people." We bop back and forth—and upward—in our path toward maturity or wisdom. Remember that the right and left sides of the helix will usually be unsolvable dilemmas, whereas each horizontal level will be solvable. This picture has helped me to visualize much of my own learning.

Now, for a different example, the second level might be the apparent paradox that we are all *unique* and yet we are all the *same*. When you have solved this paradox, you then move up another rung, and so on. Each new level presents a new problem to solve. The paradox for a fully enlightened person is that they are unlimited in mind but limited by their human form. How does one solve this paradox?

I present the helix, but I cannot populate it with actual examples, because I cannot tell you how to become wise. There are two reasons for this. First, there is no single road to wisdom. You must climb your own helix. Our unique and diverse perspectives are the only things that make life interesting. Second, even if I knew of perfect examples, I would not provide them. I don't wish to live your life for you. However, in Chapter 7, we will look at how the Periodic Table is constructed to give a clearer meaning to this zigzagging and bopping back and forth.

*Ideas about spiritual maturity*

In *The Road Less Traveled*, we read about four levels of spiritual maturity. I will explain them differently than Peck does, in order to provide something new and useful. Like everything in this book, this is not a model to *believe*. I present it as something to think about, to ponder, to consider. Stage models should always be taken with at least three grains of salt, for several reasons. First, we all have different trajectories in life, so there is no generalized path. Second, the theorists who make these models always conveniently locate themselves at the highest stage. Put simply, they desire to seem the most advanced. Third, humans are composed of hierarchical, overlapping, and inconsistent systems—meaning that we probably inhabit all four stages of spiritual maturity during a typical day. We are not so easily categorized.

*What are these stages?*

Peck presents the structure of Alcoholics Anonymous as a method for people to move their thinking from Stage 1 to Stage 2. Stage 1 is often immoral or amoral people who feed their inner animals. (A quick counterpoint: in Taoism, this person might be considered ideal. The Stage 1 person does not live by a code of conduct—especially not societal rules.) Stage 2 includes devoutly religious people. They follow morals set forth by their religions. Stage 3 is the atheist, scientist, or secular humanist. Stage 4 is the spiritual person. Peck himself is, as predicted, in this final stage.

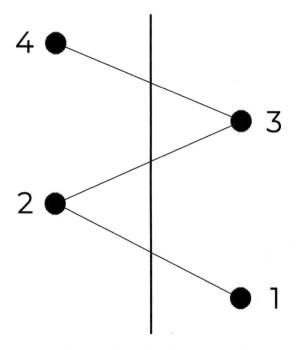

People in Stages 1 and 3 have much in common and can talk easily with one another. The same is true for people in Stages 2 and 4. However, Stages 2 and 3 cannot easily talk with one another—and most of us seem to be in Stages 2 and 3. This is exemplified by the current national debate about teaching creationism versus evolution in schools. Stage 4 thinkers, on the other hand, have little problem with both opinions carrying weight. They simply say, "Well, how about God created us through evolution?" However, we can argue that God is not necessarily the same as the word "God." In fact, the *Tao Te Ching*, the main book of Taoism, basically begins by saying, 'The God that can be labeled is not the true God.'

How else can we compare and contrast these

stages? They are all about where our principles and ideas about morality come from—where our *rules for behavior* originate. Stages 1 and 3 do not believe in rules that come from outside of humanity, while Stages 2 and 4 believe there is something at work that is greater than mere human intellect. These people typically possess a type of humility, though of course not absolute humility. It takes pride to think God created humans in his image.

tWhen people in Stages 2 and 4 use the word "God," they usually mean different things by it—but they do not usually get offended by the use of the word itself. In general, "spirituality" simply means the belief that humans possess something beyond mere intellect. Where does this "something beyond intellect" come from? Well, probably it comes from the very same place our intelligence comes from. And where is that? Nobody knows, but we have no problem admitting that we are more intelligent than most animals and plants and rocks. Our intelligence is a mystery, and our moral compass is not necessarily something that pure rationality or utilitarianism can help us with. We will discuss spirituality a bit more in the next chapter.

*What else can we envision with the helix?*

The helix can help us visualize certain patterns of causation. Most spirals go inward or outward, but we can just as easily imagine them with a height dimension instead. We have both vicious and virtuous circles. These occur when a pattern is self-reinforcing. In other words, a snowball rolling down a hill accumulates more and more snow. Its impact at the bottom will be that much bigger.

In the social arena, a virtuous circle is something where good behavior is rewarded and we begin to see more of it. A vicious circle is where bad behavior is rewarded and things keep getting worse. We are always rightly very scared of hitting slippery slopes or entering one of these whirlpools because they can gather force as they continue. A systems engineer must be especially cognizant of these factors. Even a constructed system like a bridge requires thought about avoiding self-re-inforcing causal loops—as when the Tacoma Narrows Bridge collapsed due to aeroelastic flutter.

A spiral effect just means that something has more than *direct* effects. That is, it has effects that cause further effects, which we might label *indirect*. Then either the direct or indirect effects cause yet more effects. We imagine that a spiral will occur if any country ever launches a nuclear bomb—soon we would be in WWIII. Indeed, intertwined direct and indirect effects are what led to WWI.

A less scary topic: boom-and-bust financial cycles are often spirals containing feedback loops. The 2007 financial crisis spiraled because certain derivative securities were mispriced and owned by many different institutions. If the federal government (under Obama) had not bailed out the big banks, it would have caused a domino effect, and our world would look much different today. Perhaps it *should* look different, but people tend to prefer stability to change.

A debt downgrade by a credit rating agency can cause

a downward spiral for the target company. Such effects are purely quantitative as higher equity is required. This can lead to problems with prior agreements and begin a downward spiral. However, the effects can also be reputational. Any harm to a company or person's reputation easily snowballs. People who are in positions to cause snowball effects need to be very careful of their words and actions. In my personal opinion, a celebrity should have a higher standard of behavior than a common citizen—at least while they are in the public eye. If a celebrity proves to be mean-spirited or evil, they should forfeit their right to fame. This does not mean they go to jail. It simply means they must work retail or a service job like the rest of us. Why celebrate a person who is not good?

*What are some other effects we can visualize?*

A domino effect is a different causal process from a snowball effect. With dominoes, there is only one direct effect at the very beginning, and the other effects are all indirect. The second domino through to the penultimate domino alternate between being effects and being causes. But there is a final domino. Thus, it is not a self-reinforcing pattern. It is not circular—rather, it is finite.

Cognitive scientist Tina Grotzer details a concept called "mutual causality," where cause and effect arise mutually rather than in sequence. I realized several years ago that the weather did not cause my mood. In fact, my mood and the weather were both arising from the same source: whereabouts unknown. This is an example of uniting a cause and effect into a single phenomenon. In other words, it is an argument from non-duality: there is not a separate cause and effect for everything in the universe. Many things arise mutually. Perhaps even human consciousness is emergent in this same way: a cohesive pattern that forms out of simpler interactions. No single biological factor could lead to consciousness, but all of them together somehow do.

In many ways, wisdom is about returning to a balance in our thinking about how things are different and how they are the same. We mostly only concentrate on how things differ. When we differentiate cause and effect, we may lose some important information, such as a hidden cause or a more imaginative solution. When we can integrate cause and effect into a single phenomenon, our thinking becomes more sophisticated.

In the next chapter we will continue integrating our thinking when we discuss author Eckhart Tolle's teachings on spiritualty. Like integrating cause and effect into a mutual system, we will try to integrate subject and object in a new way.

*Key Ideas*

- Our culture does not promote the idea of transcending apparent opposites.

- We can form a triangle as the solving of an apparent paradox.

- Triangles on top of one another begin to resemble a helix

- We can arrange ideas about spiritual maturity into a four-point helix.

- We must be careful of spiral causation, or feedback loops, within systems.

- Sometimes cause and effect arise mutually.


*Discussion Questions*

- Think of some problems you faced when you were younger, and see if you can graph them to a triangle or helix.

- What are some additional areas where people are confused or wrong about naming the cause versus the effect of something?

- Should celebrities be held to different standards than the rest of us? Is this fair?

# chapter seven

## *Onionology: The Pulsating Heart of Empathy*

*Overview*

We now turn our attention to the stinky, tear-inducing, lowly onion. Could any root vegetable be dirtier? Yet the onion is a fascinating and ultra-powerful shape—the best one we cover. In fact, the onion can help us reach enlightenment—but we will save that story for later in the chapter. We will call the onion Larry because he has many layers. (If we give him a descriptive name like Sir Lancelot or Robin Hood, he becomes fun and easy to recall.) Larry is a powerful shape to work with—both illuminating and versatile. He can teach us more than any other shape. (Don't tell the other shapes, but I like Larry best of all.)

Please pull out an onion as your mascot for this chapter. If you cannot find one, try to visualize a cross-section of this three-dimensional shape: an inner core surrounded by layers with increasing surface area. The onion is a common metaphor—we peel back the outer layers to reveal deeper and deeper meanings. Or we can imagine the concentric circles radiating either inward or outward.

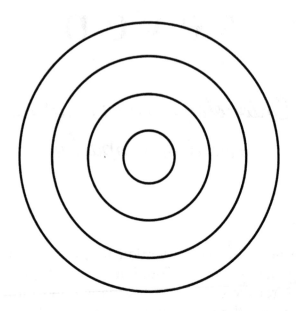

In this chapter, Larry will introduce us to many concepts: ingroups and outgroups, influence footprints, ripple effects, vertical and horizontal spirituality, the learning process, and more. Some of these concepts relate to the social world, while others relate to the inner self. We'll begin by examining how cultural values differ in the United States and Russia. We'll then discuss friendships, ingroups, and outgroups.

*Cultural values*

The zeitgeist of the 1950s—the second half of the atomic age—celebrated the shape of the atom. In Brussels, Belgium, the Atomium (an atom sculpture big enough to wander through) was constructed for the 1958 World's Fair. If you doubt that mental models possess value in the real world, you might be underestimating their power. The atom served as a visual template for social organization: specifically, the so-called "ideal family," or "nuclear family," which is also sometimes called the smallest viable unit of society. At the center, the nucleus, stand the mother and father. The orbiting electrons are the children. When this model promotes the ideal family shape, it subtly devalues different arrangements.

In the United States, we traditionally value money very highly. Indeed, people often value their work above other considerations. Historically, the cornerstone of our freedom has rested upon class mobility through hard work—our ability to transform from pauper into millionaire. However, when class mobility becomes less common, we must use different grand narratives to show how we are a free people. After money concerns, people often look toward family life for meaning. After that, we look for meaning in friendships.

My experience from living in Russia offers me a competing worldview—encountering new grand narratives is a major benefit of travel. In Russia, people strongly value friendships. Decades ago, under the Soviet system, the only way to obtain anything at all was through one's social connections. So friendships had to be quite deep. As their second priority, Russians, like Americans, value their families. Finally, in third place, Russians value work and money. These are of course generalizations, but without a stable economy, it makes sense to value one's working life less.

For historical and cultural reasons, life in different places is indeed different. If you don't like where you live, I urge you to consider moving. This is contrary to the popular idea that you bring your inner world with you no matter where you go. That idea may be true, but until you can master your inner realm, your environment is quite crucial.

Epicurus, who wrote about how to lead a happy life, ranked friendship as his highest priority. He enjoyed life, lived by this advice, and promoted it. Russian culture embraces this idea more than American culture, but we do not have to accept everything mainstream culture teaches us, as discussed in Chapter 5. Incidentally, Epicurus ate plain rice rather than rich Epicurean tidbits. His primary message has been twisted over time.

With the advent of social media, we now have access to more people than ever before. However, these connections are often shallow. Deep friendships are based on shared experience and disclosure—shared vulnerability. We possess greater power to choose our friendships than to choose our family.

*Friendships*

We all live in a sea of coworkers, family members, friends, acquaintances, and strangers. Obviously, we cannot choose the strangers we bump into, nor even most of our family members. We possess a little power over choosing our coworkers. Where we theoretically have complete control is in choosing our friends. Do we seek friends who challenge us or do we prefer friends who comfort us? Perhaps we want a mix of both.

It is crucial to our well-being to consider who we spend our time with and whether we count these people as friends. We must be honest with ourselves by allotting our precious time according to our true priorities (see Appendix B). If we spend all of our time with people who drag us down, *we* are the ones at fault—not them. While a saint may not become like the people around him or her, most of us do face this danger. On the other hand, if we don't become like the people around us in some ways, we become outcasts in our own circle. Neither of these options is ideal. In these cases, we should rebuild our friend circles.

Whom do we count as our friends? According to Bertrand Russell, "Very few people can be happy unless on the whole their way of life and their outlook on the world is approved by those with whom they have social relations... To almost everybody, sympathetic surroundings are necessary to happiness." (Russell, Ch. 9) In other words, if we disagree with our neighbors on matters of importance, we should consider relocating. Of course, before virtual communication, geography played a more crucial role in our lives. The onion was more literal. Now, however, our associates can be diasporic—like polka-dots on a map, pepperoni slices on a pizza, or the holes in Swiss cheese. Nevertheless, we can imagine our inner circles and outer layers along the ring-like dimensions of the onion. Close friends are near our core, moving outward we reach acquaintances, and at our outermost layers lie strangers who live thousands of miles away.

A lot of people emphasize these distant layers when we start to talk about empathy. How can we have a positive outlook on life when we allow faraway children to starve? Saint Augustine tells us, "Since you cannot do good to all, you are to pay special attention to those who, by the accidents of time, or place, or circumstances, are brought into closer connection with you." This is good advice for several reasons. For one thing, the "too far away" lament is often used as an excuse to do *nothing*. Some say that if we are going to practice empathy, we should help the most downtrodden. But this is a theoretical stance that gets in our way of helping the people in our immediate surroundings. Helping faraway strangers is great. But if you're not helping anyone because faraway people are starving, then you need to consider acting. Never let a hypothetical or theoretical argument sway you from practicing good with your own hands. This is sometimes called "analysis paralysis," where the perfect is the enemy of the good. Find the people around you who need your help and help them. Do not simply give them money; give them your time, attention, positive mentality, or knowledge.

## Ingroups and Outgroups

In the social world, we often identify ourselves by the groups we belong to as well as those we do not. An ingroup is the group we identify ourselves with, while the outgroup is everyone else. Sometimes these identifications are fully conscious, and other times they are subconscious. Sometimes we don't choose our associates at all—they choose us, or perhaps they simply live nearby.

As we age, our ingroup can grow or shrink. Over the course of our lives, we are like pulsating onions. A growing onion often feels good, while a shrinking onion feels terrible. When someone dies in our inner circle, we lose a piece of ourselves. A void is created where once there was a deep connection. Yet we maintain the ultimate control over whether our onion grows or shrinks. After a loss, we have the ability to choose to keep growing our onion—this shows that we will not give up.

On a somewhat superficial level, we group ourselves by various demographic data points: age, nationality, gender, income, race. Sometimes we befriend other members of the same groups, but we are not required to do this. On a deeper level, we join groups that share our particular interests or values. We like certain types of music, enjoy cooking with particular kinds of cookware, or support similar charities. Here again, we can choose our friends based on shared interests, or we can seek out people completely unlike us.

As with our discussion of foregrounds and backgrounds, one cannot form an ingroup without creating an outgroup. Psychologists have discovered several ways that we tend to treat our ingroups and outgroups differently: we tend to favor ingroup members, we align our beliefs to ingroup norms, and we feel that outgroup members are all the same while ingroup members are

125

diverse and unique. Here again, we find a nice quote from Bertrand Russell: "The idea that, although oneself is full of mysterious and impenetrable depths, other people are quite easy to understand, is part of the belief in one's own superiority which most people carry about with them in spite of its statistical improbability."

Race is just one of many attributes that people use to divide humanity. Many people visualize an "us versus them" mentality that causes them to choose one side or another. This is especially true in politics. A gain for one side is seen as a loss for the other. I urge you to see the world more as an onion, where we as individuals decide how far away from our core our layers will stretch. If we want to remain open, we let in people who are different from ourselves. If we are content to stay static, we remain closed. Of course, there are some dangers that group mentalities can bring, which we discuss now.

*The dangers of a group or tribal mentality*

When pondering our various groupings, there are three group mentalities that we must guard against: herd mentality, turf mentality, and silo mentality. "Herd mentality" refers to the bias that leads us to concur with and follow the prevailing mainstream attitudes and behaviors, as discussed in Chapter 5. This mentality appeals for reasons like safety, friendship, lack of expertise, or even sheer laziness. Motivations aside, herds form, and when they muster enough frenzy, we call them mobs.

"Turf mentality" refers to the arguments we often

see in television police dramas. For example, one police force does not want to share jurisdiction with another, so the two opposing groups either hoard information or work to sabotage one another. Turf mentality appeals to those who want sole ownership or managerial control over their work. People with turf mentality fear that the wrong person might receive credit for work, or perhaps they fear an outsider will misuse information and ruin some local scheme.

Finally, "silo mentality" obscures knowledge from outside view and is pernicious in its invisibility. While turf mentality refers to horizontal overlap, where concerned parties should possess a shared goal, silo mentality is vertical, hiding its information from other disciplines that do not share jurisdiction. The goals behind silo mentality include gate-keeping, hiding illegal activity, or keeping a power dynamic alive.

Not all silos are intentional—cultures that speak different languages represent the extreme of this mentality. Silo mentality also occurs in small ways every day. We ignore people and messages we do not understand, and we ignore those who do not under-stand *us*. Whether deliberate or the unintentional shape of the world, silo mentality, like turf mentality, thwarts cooperation across groups.


## Social media

Our modern social-media-curated lives are becom-ing a danger to independent thinking. For democracy to function, we need cooperation across different people and groups. Social media platforms at first appeared to offer the potential to connect the world through the internet. Unfortunately, a few years later, a paradox has arisen. The consumer of the Facebook feed—us—is now able to curate a bespoke news feed.

Through our own actions and those of invisible computer algorithms, we are pulled into perverse vicious cycles where the more we like a particular topic, the more that topic becomes the only thing we see. We are becoming enclosed in bubbles. We are partly to blame, and the ability of platforms like Facebook and Twitter to curate our viewing is partly to blame. But more important than casting blame is the shared need for a solution. The process has reached such epic proportions that many people who do not share our bubbles have begun to seem completely incoherent to us.

For more societal-level proof of the dangers of tribalism and group mentality, we need look no further than the 2001 Al Qaeda attack on the World Trade Center or the 2007 financial crisis. Here we see what happens when group mentalities cause systems to break down. We know that intelligence agencies suffered from both turf and silo mentalities when they refuse to translate and share their information. These mentalities will plague every discipline where information is the primary commodity. Herd mentality, on the other hand, stands at the forefront of every financial crisis with boom-and-bust cycles.

To prevent these kinds of disasters that spill far outside the guilty groups, herd mentality with creeping norms must be realigned from outside, turf mentality must give way to larger, shared goals, and silo mentality must look toward interdisciplinary sources for new ideas. We cannot curate ourselves into corners. While we often value harmony and consensus in our groups rather than independent reality checks, someone must do something to keep us connected as a species.

How do we solve all of these problems? We look to the onion. Though composed of many layers, it is a single unified vegetable. We can actively enlarge our ingroups to include more layers. Eventually our ingroup could include our enemies, then people we know nothing about. Alternatively, we could take on the role of outsider. From this perspective, we shrink our ingroup to just ourselves. The cultural outsider is more a reality in the East, where spirituality has a longer cultural history.

*The outsider perspective*

I could write an entire book about the importance of outsiders and the increasing dangers of specialization in our world—and I almost did. Frankly, I did not write that book because it was an intellectual treatise with no target audience. We do not reward outsiders. We are more likely to fear or kill them. If we are more civilized than barbarians, then we merely do not allow them a livelihood or income. Put another way, we could ask: who would pay an outsider to protect us from ourselves?

The government interferes in certain free-market inevitabilities like monopolies. Think of any particular working group, from professional to retail to manual labor. Managers must have an expertise in the work itself, yet there is often no way to reward much-needed outsider opinions. We are now observing some of the problems that arise when everyone increases their specialization or bubble with no one observing from the outside. There are both advantages and disadvantages to being an outsider. The downsides are emotional and obvious. We feel all alone in the world. To quote Bertrand one last time, "Fundamental happiness depends more than anything else upon what may be called a friendly interest in persons and things" (Russell, Ch. 10). If someone inhabits this isolated space for an extended period, we might call them antisocial. Sometimes such a person sees something wrong with everyone except themselves. Alternatively, they could have an inferiority complex. In either case, they set themselves apart from other people. This is a lonely place to inhabit.

However, outsider status is perfectly healthy when it occurs occasionally or intentionally. The upside of outsider status is a bird's-eye view of the world. When we are not embedded in systems, we can better observe how they operate. Further, we can act more dispassionately to better decide disputes, like third-party judges or arbiters. We don't want judges who are friends with the plaintiffs or the defendants. Judges are outsiders in a specific context, but when they take off their robes, they rejoin society. Few people would want to stay outsiders for long.

We now turn to another use for the onion metaphor. We examine how it can help us view the effects of our influence in the world.

*Influence and ripple effects of our actions*

We all influence the world. Every action has a repercussion. These effects can be intentional, unintentional, good, bad, or multifarious. This section explains how we can use the onion to better visualize influence, causation, and ripple effects.

A critical conversation today is regarding the scale and scope of our carbon footprints. Calculating our footprint has to do with much more than whether we recycle or not. The picture gets more complex because we must measure a huge amount of data to get the net effect for each individual. We have to examine our consumption, our waste, our actions, and our influence on other people. As the ecology mantra suggests, we must bring awareness to the total of our reducing, reusing, and recycling efforts. For example, if someone does not eat meat, does not drive a car, and does not own a house, it does not make sense to complain that they use a plastic straw. In other words, we must see the sum total of a person's carbon footprint.

Think of the expanding rings of the onion as increasing segments of time and space. The further out the rings get, the longer the time period we are investigating. Like a stone thrown into a pond, the first circle is the exact area of the stone's contact with the water. Then, the ripples move outward like rings as time elapses. If the time period is one second, we see two rings, but if we wait five seconds, we will see fifteen rings. This is literally a look at the big picture. The spatial *size* of the effect—and the time elapsed after the effect—both increase.

Keep this image in mind as we turn to the some-what famous story of the Chinese horse farmer. This a story that often appears in spirituality books. This man owned some land and a single horse. One day, his horse up and vanished. The other villagers stopped by and remarked to the farmer about his bad fortune. A few days later, the horse returned, bringing two wild horses with him. The other villagers again stopped by to remark on the farmer's good fortune. When the farm-er's son tried to tame one of the wild horses, he broke his leg. The other villagers stopped by and remarked on the farmer's bad fortune. Conscription officers then came through the village to draft all the able-bodied men into the army. They couldn't take the farmer's son because his leg was broken. The other villagers stopped by and remarked on the farmer's good fortune.

Besides pointing out some very nosy neighbors, this story illustrates how little control we have over the world. However, its main point is the serendipity of labeling things as good or bad. We can trace every action to something in the past—to before we were born. But at some point, must we not begin taking responsibility for our actions?

When we examine more precisely what is happen-ing in this story, the villagers are isolating snippets of time and space—specifically a past data point and a current data point—and then they are comparing the two to determine whether circumstances exhibited improvement or deterioration. We all do this. But from the story you can see how our judgments can never be the final word.

So, are the villagers making mistakes in their judgments? Oh yeah, I forgot to mention that in the story the Chinese farmer himself always responded to the other villagers by just saying, "Maybe." This story is supposedly about how wise he is and how foolish all the other villagers are. But are they really behaving foolishly? Perhaps they are judging prematurely, but when is the proper time to judge a thing?

Shakespeare, through his character Hamlet, claims that, "Nothing is bad or good, but thinking makes it so." In other words, the judgments we make are based on the evidence we choose to examine at any given time. Similarly, the decisions we make are based on the information we examine beforehand, both the inputs and the desired outcomes. We call a decision rational when it uses the logic of ratios—costs versus benefits—to arrive at a solution. Likewise, an emotional decision considers emotions when determining an answer. The actual results of these decisions are therefore beside the point—and largely out of our control, as we see here. What we can control, however, are the inputs and the intended outcomes that we consider.

We specify the making of wise decisions, therefore, by specifying the wise inputs and wise intended outcomes that we include in the decision-making process. Through education and imagination, this effort begins to be manageable. Appendix A will examine wise decision-making in greater detail.

As mentioned in the last chapter, a good understanding of cause and effect is crucial to wisdom. We now see that ripple effects mean that the effects of our actions go far beyond our own lifetimes!

*Alternating patterns in science and the learning process*

Remember from Chapter 2 how Dottie is the endpoint of complete differentiation. "Differentiation" is the process of separating things into their smallest components, and then naming them based upon their differences. Recall again how Adam named the various animals in Genesis. The learning process—and science in general—both possess very interesting alternating patterns of integration and differentiation. For example, we use prime numbers from mathematics to encrypt information. Without explaining exactly what they are, it is necessary to point out that prime numbers are usually considered random—thus their use in encryption. But recently, scientists discovered that the atoms in crystals are similarly arranged. Is there order in this chaos after all?

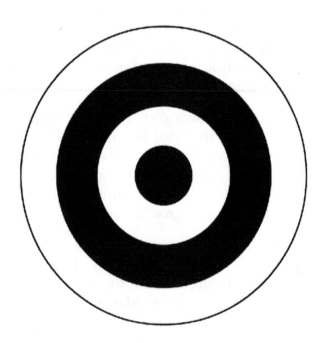

When observed from afar, science—and the learning process—both exhibit alternating patterns, a bit like the graphic on the cover of this book. Alan Watts compares this realization to using an idealized microscope. First, we look at cells, then we slowly increase the magnification of the lens, and the image blurs. In a few minutes, the next layer of individual units comes into focus. Now we see atoms. We slowly increase the magnification again through blurry images until suddenly atomic particles become clear.

In other words, what is noise and incoherence at one level becomes order at the next level. In science we have the Periodic Table as the outcome of this process over many iterations. First, we differentiate all the elements—we name them. Then we see that they are actually connected in some way—they all have electrons. Later, we see that they all are different again—they all have a different number of electrons. Then we see that we can arrange them in order into a table. In short, we differentiate and integrate back and forth until we have something extremely useful. Chaos and order alternate, depending on where our knowledge stands at any given time. The history of science alternates as it moves towardt ultimate truth, which is the outermost edges of the onion. To mix metaphors, we could say that absolute truth is *alternating turtles* all the way down. (In ancient lore, a turtle carries the flat Earth on its back. Some curious people as what lies under the turtle.)

The blur and focus modes are simply two different ways of seeing the world. The microscope was one example, but this alternating idea can be found in other places. To learn something, we move between a *diffuse* state and a *focus* state. Broadly speaking, the learning process involves labeling and categorization. "Labeling" is how things differ, and "categorization" is how they relate to one another—how they are similar. In the diffuse mode, we daydream and let the subconscious wander. In the focus state, our attention is focused upon the problem at hand. We need both states to fully understand and add to knowledge. The overworked doctoral student without the time to integrate knowledge is at best someone lacking big-picture insight, and at worst a potentially dangerous thinker.

Our education system has generally favored differentiation—the dissecting of information into its component parts. For example, we learn all the different bones of the body that together make up the skeleton. On the other hand, when we seek to integrate knowledge, we take a collection of seemingly separate parts and recast them as a single entity. Spirituality is popular in part because it focuses on this neglected half of the world. It is very important for people to realize where *they* connect and how *they* are similar to other people.

*Identity onions*

The onion can also help us visualize our own identities. An identity is a claim of what one is as well as what one is not. Our identities often encompass demographic data, our goals, our livelihoods, etc. Of course, many of us extend ourselves with material possessions.

A claim to geographic location, or GPS coordinates, is the clearest analogy to an onion. Those close to you are literally close to you in distance, and they

136

might be close to you figuratively, based on how much you care for them. A maternal bond is in no small part based on nine months at the exact same location.

Think about our neighbors. I live in Oregon; I thus have something in common with everyone else who lives here. I am from the United States; I recognize the borders of this country. I am an American. I am an Earthling. I orbit the Sun. I am in the Milky Way galaxy. Ultimately, I should be able to find common ground—quite literally—with anyone on the planet. We can make friends of geographical convenience, or, in the internet era, we can choose certain characteristics we value and find someone all the way across the globe who matches. And ultimately, our ingroups and outgroups do not have to be people.

We'll discuss this further at the end of the chapter when we examine horizontal spirituality. For now, we'll move to vertical spirituality, which foregrounds consciousness as the most important aspect of the universe. We must always foreground something when we think and act. Hence, there is never one universal answer for everything.

*What spiritual moves can we make with Larry the Onion?*

The onion can help us see who we truly are. Often we identify by our nationality, race, political party, age, occupation, and perhaps our choice of material possessions. The further these things are from the center of the onion, the less important they are to our identities. Thus, it is a good practice to map out our various affiliations and mark how closely we hold on to them. Start

137

with things like how you introduce yourself to a stranger. Are you your job, for example?

After mapping out the things we attach to our identities, we can begin to question the power these things have over us. Do we want every little thing about our identity to hold power over us? How far inside the onion can we get? Can we get to the very inner core? And if we do, what will we find?

Are we our possessions? If we lose our house or our car, are we still alive? When we lose our livelihood, many of us fall into depression. But hopefully we eventually realize that even our professions do not define us.

Are we our beliefs? Can we change our beliefs and stay alive? Most people actually find that changing their beliefs is liberating rather than imprisoning. In other words, the smaller our core identity, the more power we have. Our personal power becomes immune to outside circumstances—which is liberating.

Are we our bodies, or do we simply *use* our bodies? Are we our thoughts? We can observe our thoughts, so they are not actually *us*. When my mother died in front of me, her spirit left instantly. The dead body that lay there no longer held any interest for me. I don't know *where* she went, but she certainly wasn't still stuck in that dead body. Even my father, who loved her *and* her body, went and sat down across the room. We are not our bodies. We are also not our egos.

The main thrust of most spiritual practice is a process called "ego decentering." (For the materialistic person, the ego is the center of their being.) Decentering can be achieved using various methods, such as spatial, temporal, or linguistic. We already learned that whenever a statement is made, a duality is created. Because one thing is always foregrounded, something else is always backgrounded. Thus, our language never corresponds directly with truth. By examining underlying assumptions, we can critique any theory. It is particularly fruitful to analyze a writer's own biases, as ethicist Carol Gilligan does with Lawrence Kohlberg's placement of abstract principles in moral reasoning at the pinnacle of his stage model of development.

The background is often an overlooked underlying assumption. In fact, we can always try to invert our own lens to think more creatively. For example, we only know our finitude because we recognize that there is something eternal. Spirit is often a forgotten background in the West, but in this section, we foreground it.

The concept of wisdom historically foregrounds time. The older someone is, the wiser they are—at least by comparison to their younger self. But what happens if we background time and foreground space? We gain wisdom not as a self, examining our own and others' experiences over time, but by moving our attention to the present moment. We can move our attention wherever we want, though this practice is difficult in distracting environments. We develop wisdom through shifting our attention and perspective outside of the mind. The deliberate movement of attention along spatial dimensions ties together some diverse ideas toward development, including Eckhart Tolle's vertical spirituality, spiritual teacher Michael Kalton's horizontal spirituality, and our primal sensory awareness.

*Eckhart Tolle's vertical spirituality*

We now dis-identify ourselves from our own minds—our thoughts and emotions. Tolle encourages us to pursue subject-object differentiation and integration *now*, using spatial language that supplants the need for yet more time. "Subject-object differentiation" simply means pulling away pieces from yourself that you thought were a part of you. For example, if you think you are your job, then your job is part of your subject. But when you dis-identify with your job— perhaps by losing it—your job becomes a mere object that you can observe. The process of chipping away at such outward identities is decreasing the size but increasing the power of what you call *you*. In short, the subject is the observer, while the object is the thing that is observed. If you can see it, touch it, observe it, then it isn't *you*.

This differs slightly from the traditional development theories that we looked at in Chapter 4 because those required time. Tolle, a spiritual teacher and author, is primarily concerned with the *depth* (or *height*) of experience that is available to individuals when they stop identifying themselves with their beliefs. Awareness is that ability which allows us to observe our own thoughts and feelings. For Tolle, conscious thoughts and labels are aspects of the ego; the spiritual goal is to dissolve the ego, thus allowing one's true nature to emerge. "You are the light of Presence, the awareness that is prior to and deeper than any thoughts and emotions." (Tolle 2005, p. 117–8) For example, a thought perceives the notion of a tree, an abstraction, while awareness perceives every tree as the unique entity that it is. Tolle teaches us that by dissolving one's ego, one acquires a powerful and personal peace. While the nonmaterial realm is most important to Tolle, he still teaches us to honor the material world, not to disavow it or ignore it. Jung also advised this. They both understand that to background something too often means to hide it.

Tolle teaches that the ego is never satisfied. It seeks to complete itself in the future, which of course never comes, for completion is only available in the present moment. Since the ego lives through past and future, the answer to overcoming it is to live in the present moment—the eternal now. When time itself no longer exists, the three dimensions that remain define space. One of Tolle's most repeated admonitions in dealing with a perceived problem is to "give it space."

Giving space is a process that entails several distinct steps. When we give a problem space, we are creating a gap between our direct experience and our reaction to it. When we decouple our experiences and our reactions, we are in effect withholding judgment on whether an experience is good or bad. The longer the gap is between experience and reaction, the more empowered we become to choose our reaction free from the bonds of habit and conditioning. Lengthening this gap leads us to realize that we can choose our thoughts. It is not an *experience* that is positive or negative, rather it is our *interpretation* of an experience that categorizes it.

Next in the process, we can give space to the gap between interpretation and emotion. It's natural to match our emotions to our interpretations; after all, emotions are tools we use to help guide our actions. However, when this gap is lengthened, we find that choosing our emotions independent of our interpretations becomes possible, just as choosing our interpretations independently of our experiences in the earlier step became possible.

Addressing this second gap, psychologist Lisa Barrett states: "Which emotion is experienced, and how it is experienced, is a matter of intentional focus and interpretation." While Tolle speaks in terms of spirituality, academic research on consciousness corroborates his theory: "This view—that an experience of emotion is a state of mind whose content is at once affective (pleasant or unpleasant) and conceptual (a representation of your relation to the world around you)—is consistent with recent theoretical insights in the neurobiology of consciousness." (Barrett et al., 2007, p. 386, 389)

To engage in this process, we must use our wills or spirits to their fullest extent. The end result is a form of Buddhist nonattachment, however we might stop to question this ultimate goal. Zen essayist R. H. Blyth spent many years perfecting his own nonattachment but ultimately decided to do the opposite: he got as attached as possible to as many things and people as he could. The grand pendulum tends to swing as we strive for the proper balance in life. Tolle often ignores the scope and scale of the subconscious, relying on a method that can shape only the thoughts and feelings that we are aware of. Whereas for Jung, delving into the subconscious is necessary to fully integrate ourselves.

In Tolle's spirituality, we are creating space by distancing ourselves from the experiential world into our highest connection with consciousness itself—a metaphorically vertical move. This is distinguished from horizontal spirituality, which we now turn to.

142

*Horizontal spirituality*

In this section we explore horizontal spirituality—which we could also call "radical ecology" or simply "green living." We begin with a poem:

Think long term.

Embrace with joy the changing seasons.

Be content with your natural beauty.

Let your limbs sway and dance in the breezes.

Be flexible.

Remember your roots."

—*Advice from a Tree*, Ilan Shamir

Horizontal spirituality examines the systemic interdependency of everything in the world's environment. Because we need things like oxygen, gravity, flora, and fauna to survive, these seemingly external factors are actually very much a part of us. Green spirituality focuses on our interaction with plants and animals and reacts against the anthropocentrism of human history. Instead of a hierarchical view of nature, green spirituality urges us to consider the short history of humankind in the world. According to horizontal spirituality teacher Michael Kalton, "Long-term survivors seem to be simple life forms such as blue-green algae, rather than complex organisms such as dinosaurs or humans. The message is clear: we have not always been here, need not be here, and almost certainly will not be here…" (Kalton 2000, p. 191)

Kalton critiques the very idea of vertical spirituality. If we posit consciousness as the ultimate origin of the world, human consciousness takes prime place, and as a result, ethics, rationality, and human understanding emerge as the highest good. However, "If we can recognize matter as alive when it is at the complex level of metabolic and self-reproductive processes, what are we to think of it at less complex levels?" (Kalton 2000, p. 198)

Kalton doesn't provide explicit prescriptions for development, but he implies that potential development exists by increasing our circle of awareness into this horizontal dimension. He moves our attention to the way the world might look from nonhuman perspectives. What can we learn by looking at the world from the perspectives of the trees, the bugs, even inert matter? Certainly our perceptions of time and scale would change, if not our behaviors.

Again, we can draw the onion's concentric circles to map out how we think about the various artifacts in our environment. Some people's outer circle would include animals, some plants, and still others the planet itself. A few astronauts with personal experience might even be able to include the moon within their ingroup, though we know too little about anything farther than that to earnestly identify with it.

In addition to practicing vertical or horizontal spirituality, we can also decenter our ego very quickly by caring more about other people. Empathy is excellent for getting our ego out of the way. And after many years of ego decentering, it comes very naturally. Helping others has many rewards: you feel needed, useful, purposeful, and not overly worried about your own problems.

In sum, we discuss these various types of integrative thinking because they show us how to look at the knowledge we already possess in new ways. In our world of information overload, we rarely need *more* information, but we do need better ways to organize and direct the information we have.

*Sensory awareness*

In addition to shifting our attention vertically and horizontally, we can shift our attention to our sense perceptions. Instead of living in mindful awareness, we can live in sensory awareness. While we possess five main senses, we can often add additional senses to this repertoire. We can learn to differentiate our emotions, we can learn how to dance and move our bodies, we can listen to the ways our bodies communicate with us. We can discern rhythm, mood, pitch, and many other things that do not get a lot of research. While this book talks about thinking, remember that it is but one small part of our lives. It can be a great director, but it is not the only member of the cast.

*Key Ideas*

- Life is different in different places. People value things differently across the world.

- We can choose our friends.

- If we see suffering around us, we should help. The fact that people are starving in a faraway country does not give us an excuse to do nothing at home.

- We can use the onion to visualize our ingroups and outgroups. The world is not full of warring tribes but simply people you identify less with.

- Groups are susceptible to herd mentality, turf mentality, and silo mentality.

- Outsiders are crucial to a functioning society, but we do not have a system that pays for or honors their opinions.

- We must examine the ripple effects we cause through time and space.

- Science and the learning process both follow alternating patterns we could call "order" and "chaos."

- Spirituality is about ego-decentering.

- We are a lot less and yet a lot more than we tend to think we are.

- We do not have to react, and we can choose our emotions. Yes, it takes work.

- Humans are not necessarily the *goal* of the universe.

- We can bring more attention to our sense perceptions.

*Discussion Questions*

- How is the alternating onion concept similar to binary? To dialectics?

- Do you prefer vertical or horizontal spirituality and why?

- How could we pay or remunerate outsiders to keep our various systems in check?

- What additional grand narratives do you know?

- What alternating patterns do you see in the world?

- Where else could we use the idea of layers of awareness?

# chapter
# eight

*Donna Matrix and Communication*

*Overview*

We now turn to our final shape, the matrix, to discuss how to augment our limited human language and other communicative abilities. We open with a brief imaginary scenario where we communicate with space aliens. After that, we discuss three common uses for what I call a "communication matrix": simultaneous information, meta-information, and indexing. We conclude by discussing two common uses of indexing and meta-information that we are all familiar with: numbers and punctuation marks (i.e., interrobangs and question marks).

This chapter asks you to use your imagination. I do not provide specific answers to the following problems, but I do think these tools are useful to think about. While we can write some ideas down, the main point is to consider these ideas in the context of our attempts at communication.

*Empathy with space aliens*

On a clear summer day, a silver flying saucer hovers over the city. A thunderous voice rings out: "People of Earth... We have an urgent message for you..." We see a bright flash of light and the spaceship disappears. On the sidewalk, a small group gathers to peer at the sky, awaiting the message.

We have witnessed a rare example of alien communication. If you have ever watched the science-fiction movie *Arrival*, you know that aliens are presumed to speak differently than we do. In this movie's first contact, we meet two aliens that look like giant octopi floating in a dense fog. To communicate, their tentacles spray a kind of ink that forms wispy circles in the air that slowly blow away. This is their language, and no one on Earth can decipher it. Some serious complications arise, but eventually a linguist decodes the circular language.

Aliens are highly unlikely to speak English—or look like Spock—when they contact us. In fact, not only will their language use different words, but it will be, well, totally *alien*.

*(Spoilers for* Arrival *follow, so skip to the next paragraph if you want to enjoy the movie.)*

The circular alien language of *Arrival* presents information, but it also presents new perspectives. Most interestingly, the language of wispy ink circles is itself circular, rather than linear, with respect to time. Thus, these aliens discuss the past, present, and future as one and the same—they do not distinguish between them. The important discovery at the end of the film is that learning this alien language actually alters humans' perception of time. Thus, by speaking "alien," we are able to live in the past, present, and future.

This helps to give us an outsider's perspective on the English language. What does it teach us about English, or human language in general? English— including ASL (American Sign Language)—is linear. We speak, sign, and write words that can only be understood from beginning to end. A sentence can change its grammar and put clauses in any order, but we will read the sentence from left to right—from the capital letter until the period.

In the flying saucer example at the beginning of this section, the flash of light was the full communication. Everything the aliens wished to say was delivered. Thus, their style of communication is an info- or data-dump—a form of communication that does not require much time. We humans use info-dumps quite often. This book is an example. It took time to write, and it takes time to read, but it is delivered in an instant.

Let us now meet the star of this chapter, Donna Matrix. She illustrates the concepts of nonlinear communication and meta-information. She is an alien from outer space, but luckily, she understands a bit of English. Since humans never have a *fully* shared context, canon, or dictionary, our first step in communication is always to set this up. The matrix helps us with that.

151

*What is a matrix?*

A matrix is an important tool from mathematics. Drawn on paper, it looks like a box with brackets on the left and right sides. Inside are rows and columns of numbers or other types of information.

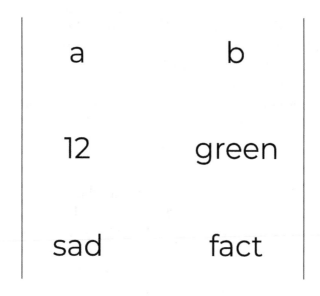

In the matrix above, we can see that the first two items are *letters*, the third item is a *number*, and the fourth item is a *color*. We can assign any meaning to these items. Perhaps they describe a picture or an opinion. They could also be a warning of some kind—say, if green was a cautionary signal. If the fourth item could be either green or blue, we could also construct a second matrix on top of this one that specified all potential values. The emotion communicated here is *sad*, but the speaker also considers it to be a *factual* communication.

The first crucial aspect of the matrix is that all the information contained in it occurs *simultaneously*. For example, a matrix typically consists of equations that describe a system. Clearly, a system where many transactions occur at one time is complex. A computer could digest complex information in an instant, but as humans, we might label the matrix an info-dump—too much for us to handle.

However, as discussed in the previous section. we often use various kinds of info-dumps. A book represents an accepted and common type. We tacitly understand that all the information in a book is handed to us in one dose. Likewise, when the boss hands us a stack of papers to be read by quitting time, that's an info-dump. In some cases, we like the convenience of an info-dump; in other cases, we do not.

What about oral communication? When we speak too fast, even a computer might complain about information overload. Have you ever given or received an oral info-dump? Consider a mother who has not spoken with her child in several weeks. "Hello, Dearie. So, two weeks ago this and that happened…and then this morning this and that happened…" She provides her child with the play-by-play commentary of her life since they last spoke. Before Dearie can even say "hello," she has given a page worth of information.

Thus, Donna Matrix reminds us that sometimes info-dumps are agreeable, and sometimes they are too much. To avoid overloading someone else, we bring awareness to what the end goal of our communication is. A conversation should be like passing a ball back and forth, while a speech is like juggling solo. Be cautious if you tend to confuse conversations with speeches. In our daily interactions, we usually need to slow down and refrain from info-dumping. For example, be authentic with your barista when you order your morning latte. Connect with your parents when you talk on the phone. Remember that good conversation is like improvisation—not scripted. When you are well-paced and authentic, chances are good you will get the same consideration in return.

While we are on the subject of info-dumping, you might have encountered the term "truth-dumping." This phrase has a negative connotation, even though it may sound like a good idea to be truthful. Radical Honesty is a movement that enjoins us to always be truthful in our communications. However, we still maintain a lot of freedom and judgment with how we speak our truth. If the truth we dump is solely meant to hurt somebody, we might reconsider our motives. In my opinion, we can stay both tactful and honest. Of course, the best truths for us to tell are the ones that set us free.

Donna Matrix proposes that we now turn our attention to her second ability: communicating meta-information.

*What is meta-information?*

In-person communication usually conveys a combination of sensory and verbal information. In fact, studies suggest that only 30 percent of our social communication is verbal. We can think of meta-information as the embodied supplement to our spoken words. Thus, in addition to transmitting words when we speak, we use ancillary and body language to convey things like our current mood and our attitude toward what we are saying. We could consider everything other than the actual information we communicate to be meta-information—or information *about* information. This stuff is under our control, but it is usually somewhat unconscious—often backgrounded. In this section, we foreground it and learn to harness its power.

"Meta" means outside or a level above or below something. In computer programming, metadata gives information *about* the program, but is not part of the program's actual functioning. Metadata provides details like authorship, date of creation, date of last update, etc. In research, a meta-analysis is an analysis that does not use raw data from its own study—it uses the results of multiple other studies.

Footnotes to a text are another type of meta-information. Hashtags in Twitter are meta. In digital music libraries, we use fields for things like genre, rating, and mood. In blogs, we use tags for subject matter. These are both meta. The concept of *categorization* often underlies meta-information—meaning meta-information exists so that we can categorize the actual information. Meta is thus abstract and conceptual. Certain other animals can also categorize things in this way, including primates, dogs, bears, and pigeons.

For a clear example of meta-information, let us turn to photography. (Since we all take selfies, this context is also practical.) Every time we snap a picture on our phones, a photograph is saved as a file. But additional information *about* the photo is also saved in this file. This information includes the image size—the number of megapixels, quality, or canvas size—as well as the GPS tag where the photo was taken, focal point, framerate, lens diameter, lighting, camera device, and time of creation. These are all meta because they are not part of the photo itself.

*How can we use meta-information to communicate better?*

Do you ever get dismayed that you cannot add certain caveats to the things you say? For example, sometimes I want to tell someone, "I say this out of tough love. I know you don't want to hear it, but it is only for your sake that I say it." Or: "Take this particular advice I am giving you with a grain of salt. I am not completely sure of your situation, but this is something that was useful to *me*." Or: "What I am asserting is my opinion. I do not regard it as fact. I only read it the other day as an idea." Or: "I have a 40 percent certainty that this opinion is correct." Or: "Don't listen to the words I'm saying. I am merely making conversation with you because I love you." Of course, adding such warnings or supplements to every sentence can get old fast. We cannot preface every statement in real life, but wouldn't it be useful?

Transactional psychology has waned in popularity, but it presents a simple and clear framework to consider how we think and how we talk to other people. According to this framework, we act out three primary roles in life: child, parent, and adult. We were all once children. In general terms, children believe in fairy tales and imaginary worlds, and they do not understand responsibility because they are cared for by a provider. Parents guide children, telling them what they should do and not do. They are particularly nosy, because children need rather complete guidance. Adults, on the other hand, take responsibility for themselves and expect others to do likewise. Throughout our lives we switch the roles we play with people through the aging and maturation processes. But we can also switch roles consciously. Often, we can play all three roles in the course of a single day.

This framework becomes insightful when we discover that we are playing the wrong roles in certain situations—we play outdated roles or simply inappropriate ones. The child must eventually grow up and take responsibility. The parent must eventually let the child become an adult. The adult must have empathy yet stay true to him or herself. In short, the child takes orders, the parent gives orders, and the adult self-orders. Thus, an adult who justifies their behavior by blaming other people is playing the role of child.

Typically, as children, we relate to our parents as children. After about eighteen years, we begin to treat them like other adults. Finally they reach old age, and in a role reversal, we become their parents. We can consider what role we play in every conversation. This role becomes a part of the meta-information we communicate, but we do not necessarily want to say it out loud to the other people. It is for our own understanding.

When we expand this framework, we can imagine that life itself is like a theatrical play with additional roles for each of us to play. When do we play the student? When do we play the prude? When do we play the butler? As long as we are aware of what role we are trying to play, we're rolling. If you play some creative characters, please let me know. You are not bound to anyone else's system. Play as an adult, or create a unique role for your life! In all of these cases, you simply add entries to the matrix that explain what role you're playing and when.

Now that we understand some general types of communication, we can get more specific. We'll examine other ways to use Donna Matrix by adding meta-information and further backgrounding to our communications. We will start with some simple binary options.

*Tagging sentences*

The metadata that we put into the matrix helps us to sort and categorize our communication. It helps us predefine words (sometimes words have generational differences) and add caveats to our communications—making the things we say more precise. We do this to meet people in their own language, in their own context—to "bridge the gap," as it were. Common language gaps include regional, cultural, generational, and educational gaps.

At its heart, the matrix is a thinking tool. It helps us determine our target audience and specify what we are really trying to say. Binary meta-information can help us communicate better. For example, is your sentence concrete or abstract? Is it an opinion or a fact? Are you conveying information or just bullshitting? In addition to these binary options, we can add certain qualifiers to our sentences. What if we are uncertain about something we say? We might begin with actually saying we are 25 to 50 percent certain. Have you ever heard anyone specify this in a speech? Recent research suggests that even dolphins can rate their certainty levels to some extent.

Language only accounts for 30 percent of our communication, but even so it is rarely clear. The words we use are never quite correct and never convey the full picture. Yet creating awareness of this problem is half the battle. There are philosophers who study semantics, but even they are still in the early stages of analyzing our semantic cues.

*Emotions and sense perceptions*

It is often appropriate to express or communicate your emotions to someone. But you can also put your emotions into a matrix to help you sort them out before discussing them. Indeed, we possess various abilities that psychologists often study regarding emotions, but we almost never learn these formally: emotional management, emotional differentiation (the ability to specify multiple emotions), and reading the emotions of others. We do not have often have classes on thinking or parsing emotion, but such classes would be very useful.

In lieu of coursework, think about the emotions you feel and add emotional language to your communications. In general, the more emotions you can name, the better. Complex emotions like nostalgia—where there are good and bad feelings—are particularly interesting to consider.

Finally, we can also add sensory perceptions to our communication needs. A human being can be thought of as a huge simultaneous system—just like a matrix. Our body language and tone of voice account for 70 percent of our communication with other people. Think about how you might communicate sensory information to other people.

*Indexing*

Indexing is one particular way of categorizing information. Consider numbers with two or more digits. We will examine the number 423. These numbers are indexed, but we do not usually remember this fact from childhood. In this case, the index is invisible, but it tells us that the order of these numbers is important. This number could not be written 234. That is a different number, even though it contains the same digits. The index is based on the decimal system, starting with the right side of the number, rather than with words, where we always start on the left side. The rightmost digit is in the 1s place, the next digit is in the 10s place, and the third digit is in the 100s place.

Now that we see how this works with numbers, you can imagine how we might use it to add indexing information to a matrix.

*Punctuation as meta-information*

Our last example of meta-information is punctuation. We all know how this works: a sentence ends at a period, and a question ends with a question mark. The interrobang is a question mark on top of an exclamation point, and there are certainly times we would want to use that. In the past, every written word was separated by a dot, but we gradually decided that was superfluous, so the [space] became yet another type of meta information for the reader.

*Giving feedback*

We end this chapter with a note on giving feedback to someone. Giving and receiving feedback are both underdeveloped skills. What is the proper way to give feedback? First, we need to label the advice as feedback. This prevents us from giving unwanted advice and prepares the recipient for what is coming.

What is most important in receiving feedback? We must recognize the intention of the feedback. We usually take it personally, but this is not often a useful tactic to employ.

*Key Ideas*

- Our language is linear.

- Meta-information is an invisible layer above or below the information we communicate.

- We should examine our emotions and learn how to communicate them well.

- We can index things inside a matrix. This creates a second layer of meta-information.

- We use meta-information all the time when we use punctuation marks.


*Discussion Questions*

- How can I explain "indexing" better?

- What other types of meta information do we use on a daily basis?

- Does meta-information have to be invisible?

- How can we use the idea of a matrix to express emotions better?

# chapter
# nine

## When Systems Collide — The Outsider — Incentives

We live our lives embedded within multiple systems, all governed by very different rules. Each system we live within—including our own bodies—leads to different way of deciding things. While we might champion democracy, that is only a small part of our world.

The largest system that we partially control is our planet's ecosystem, or what we might call the environment. This chapter focuses on this important system first, then we move on to examine smaller systems, such as business organizations and human bodies. Some of these systems are emergent, meaning no one fully designed them before they appeared—sometimes patterns simply emerge out of complexity. Alas, most systems are far beyond our ability to fully comprehend.

In Chapter 7, we briefly touched upon the importance of the outsider figure. The inauguration of

respected outsiders is becoming crucial to our continued survival within these various systems.

## The system of Earth

The "tragedy of the commons" is a fundamental
economic concept that tells us about perverse incentives. When there is a free public good, every individual has a motive to use as much of it as possible, until the
public good has been ruined—for example, overfishing.
This helps explain why governments and rules must
initially be enacted. Indeed, our country's free-market capitalism is not a natural phenomenon but must
be maintained by a governmental outsider in order
to preventing monopolies, collusion, price fixing, and
other problems that an unbridled free market would
create.

"Systems thinking" is about as complex a topic as
the human mind can handle. The interplay of *multiple* systems is that much more complex and intractable. Practically speaking, Earth is the biggest system
we live in. We can easily count the number of human
beings who have ever moved beyond Earth's atmo-
sphere. Even on Earth, it's hard for us to imagine 7
billion people or comprehend how that number differs
from 12 billion or 1 billion. But Earth certainly knows
the difference. We all know there is a limited amount of
oil and gold and fresh water; otherwise we would not
be willing to pay for it. But we sometimes forget that
there are also very limited temperatures that we need
to live within.

An outsider to a system is a person not embedded

within the system. Obviously when we are discussing the earth's environment, there are no actual outsiders. So, we must fabricate a mock outsider—someone who gets paid to bring bad news. In short, we need a whistle-blower, a truth-teller. But who would reward or pay such a person? And where would we find this person since we are all embedded on Earth?

## The megatrends within our systems

Our various systems offer many different incentives that encourage a variety of behaviors. First, we encourage specialization. Specialization as a career path began in earnest during the Industrial Revolution, when assembly lines allowed a person to perform the same action thousands of times a day. Today we have medical and scientific specializations that pay more the more you learn. The monetary benefits accruing to various specialists are so commonly understood, I need not elaborate. Yet the outsider is by nature a non-specialist. The outsider is not in the inner circle, not a member of a guild or a union member. We do not reward generalists. How could we, when all the money is controlled by the guilds? Of course, some of these specialists could double as generalists elsewhere, but that would require them to forego their lucrative specializing time. The problem is quite intractable because when we as patients have a specific ailment, we would always rather see a specialist for that than a generalist.

Second, we encourage choosing teams. In the American political system, a politician must often choose to be Republican or Democrat. Very few individuals manage to gain much traction without these group resources. They would have to be either rich or famous—and likely both. Being either loud or extreme gets media attention, and media attention is almost always good for a politician. The media shares guilt here in what news they choose to report. But they are incentivized based on ratings, and arguments and extremism bring better ratings. Perhaps viewers simply cannot resist the experience of negative emotion. Thus, the final guilty party is the individual who pays attention to verbal boxing matches. Perhaps our only alternative is to cultivate a quiet wisdom. We all quite literally had better cool it, because we cannot all move to Mars. I hope this book is helping you along your path toward cool wisdom.

Third, our own psychology encourages us to live in self-selected bubbles. Here social media comes to aid us in creating our own little Edenic echo chambers, where our favorite thoughts get repeated back to us ad infinitum. The things we are interested in are noticed by Google and Facebook. The more we click on the things we like, the more of these things they will show us, until, finally, we like everything we see! Too bad this curation is an artificial bubble. We become like the archetypical sheltered child—like Gautama Buddha, who had never in his childhood witnessed suffering. Why is this a problem? The sheltered child does not know how to play with other children and gets traumatized at the first sign of danger. We can already see this beginning with the way conservatives and liberals have begun to interact with one another. Neither side is quite sure the other is completely sane.

With all this talk of problematic incentives, we can draw an analogy to the group problems recounted in

168

Chapter 7. We can imagine climate change as a creeping norm, and the various countries as the individual members of the group. The previous solution was an outsider, but who lives outside of national borders?

## National systems

Now let us take a look at the next largest system that we inhabit: the federal government. While super-national organizations like the United Nations exist, the United States does not recognize their sovereignty (meaning they cannot tell us what to do). Furthermore, our government—even at the federal level—is not easy to classify as either a democracy or republic. In fact, it is an experimental hybrid. A pure democracy would be susceptible to mob rule, as in the French Terror, where the frequent changing of public opinion resulted in frequent beheadings. Many people got decapitated during that time, because the majority can rule against the minority at any moment, and coalitions changed so quickly that anyone could become part of a minority overnight. At that time, politicians also cared—they were not merely professional office-holders. We thus modified our governmental structure to ensure us certain individual human rights. Further, America is a *representative* democracy, meaning we elect representatives who vote for us. However, when asked how these representatives are chosen, we fall down a rabbit hole—for it is not by popular vote. And we cannot change the electoral college system by popular vote either. If you look at the Wikipedia entry for "republic," you can see how complicated this all is.

This is not a civics lesson, so we now turn to political parties. Some people think a third major political party would be a good idea. The small probability of this happening can be modeled using game theory and statistics. How do the current parties form? Just as we recreate reality every day, political parties are in a constant state of flux and theoretically could vanish tomorrow. If everyone agreed to do something, it would happen. The problem is that the current structures benefit certain people, and the people with the power will not give it up. Sociology becomes psychology. That said, Bernie Sanders was independent from either major party for a long time, and he rose to great prominence, so it is possible. This is why the establishment Democrats treated him unfairly in 2016—to their eventual dismay. Yet again, we see how poorly people treat outsiders.

How do coalitions form? Watch the Iowa Caucus to see it in microcosm. You can imagine a similar process step-by-step: a large room full of people, several of them talking at once, people listening and walking to and fro, small crowds here, a bigger crowd there, popcorn spilled on the floor. When the buzzer sounds, the person with the biggest crowd wins. You can imagine what they would be talking about: taxes, roads, schools, Citizens United (a Supreme Court ruling that greenlights large-scale corruption). The point is, you can build your own coalition right where you live. Politics truly begins at the local level—indeed, the individual level.

The political system is complex and facing many challenges. Various interest groups help to write legislation and often target certain parts of a system while ignoring others. The main benefit of a two-party system is that the winner often represents 50 percent of the voting public. The drawbacks are obvious: we only get two choices. One additional problem, of course: the parties are not themselves democracies—though to win they would likely want to imitate this form of government.

## Corporations and organizations

The next smallest system we study could be a state or a public company like Apple—it depends upon the framework we utilize to measure size—which we will cover in Chapter 11. But do we actually spend all of our time in the *government*? If we are looking for the most important systems around us, our families play a much larger role in our lives than politicians. And our workplaces play large roles as well.

Many corporate hierarchies are shaped like a tree. While most jobs outside the military allow you to go home at the end of your shift, we spend an average of forty-five hours a week taking orders. Corporations are far from democracies, yet they have their own problems with governance, such as the Peter Principle: everyone is promoted to their personal level of incompetence. Corporations are hierarchical and dictatorial from the top down. However, boards of directors are chosen by the owners (shareholders) and thus selected based on an ownership model where 1 share = 1 vote, which is a form of plutocracy.

According to philosopher Bertrand Russell, "Different types of organization bring different types of indi-

viduals to the top, and so do different states of society."
For example, families are a type of organization. From a
child's point of view, they are dictatorships. Sometimes
parents co-rule by being dictators in different realms.
Children see their parents as dictators, while spouses—
if they are lucky—have a more equal partnership. When
children grow up, they are free to leave the dictatorship
and begin their own.

## Nature's systems

The human body is a system that we only partially control. Most of us have executive control functions
in our brains, but we still have subconscious rulers. Our
bodies are also subject to disease and death. Often we
do not intuitively understand our bodies. For example,
we become more robust in adulthood when our childhood immune systems experienced greater stress. Of
course, too much immune system stress kills us. We
also seem to possess a spirit—whether this is separate
from the brain, no one knows, but we all tacitly accept
its existence. Imagine how a person who did not believe
in spirit would behave. They would appear either ridic-
ulous or evil—or both. In other words, we all assume
other people have agency and motivations; otherwise
no one would ever hang out with us. Political theorist
Hannah Arendt called evil "banal"—meaning that evil
actions arise from simplifying the world into something
uninteresting, flat, and lifeless. Perhaps to be good,
then, is to appreciate the complexity and importance of
life.

The Judeo-Christian God is often called a monarch—

not a democrat at all. But in the United States, we do not believe in monarchies, so spirituality becomes the new religion. In spirituality, we can project whatever motives we wish upon our god. And in fact, all of these systems—including monarchy—are subject to revolution.

Why is it important to see the various systems in operation around us? Precisely because they are neither stable nor permanent. If we can imagine better ways, then we should speak up. Nature, on the other hand, seems to work through universal laws that we discover through hard science.

We must know what rules each system uses in order to gain freedom from them. Knowledge is power, and we are confined by our systems until we know the rules. All these systems are interdependent, simultaneous, overlapping, and open. Enlightenment can only be found through radical independence after our realization of utter dependence. For example, I play the violin. Should people applaud when I play a nice tune? The violin was not crafted by me, the violin was not invented by me, the song was not composed by me, music itself was not invented by me, I did not teach myself to play, the violin did not simply appear in my lap one day. I must ask how many people are responsible for my playing, and it seems to be in the thousands, and likely more. Thus, my playing is a very small part of the performance. This realization brings me humility.

But what of the future? I can influence thousands of people in the ways I choose to live my life: the decisions I make, the people I care for, the new ideas I try to spread. We become a necessary part of the life-chain. Our decisions matter, and we should take care to make

173

them as wisely as we can. We want other people to enjoy what we have. We cannot hide our abilities and fail to participate. We must steward a better world in whatever ways we are able.

*Key Ideas*

- We live within multiple systems every day.

- Our systems encourage specialization.

- Our systems encourage choosing teams.

- Social media enables us to construct artificial bubbles.

- Nations and politics are systems with various rules.

- Corporations are not generally democratic.

- The human body is composed of multiple systems.

- Nature and God do not generally follow democratic principles.

- Part of the joy in life is using what other people have created. Our responsibility is to continue the life-chain and spread our own ideas and abilities.

*Discussion Questions*

- How can we open our minds to learn about the systems we live with?

- What additional types of systems were not mentioned in this chapter?

- What idea can you change today that would impact the people around you?

# c h a p t e r
# t e n

## Gestalt Perceptual Biases

*Overview*

In this chapter we talk about perceptions. To psychologists, this means our sensory perceptions, such as seeing, hearing, and feeling. Perceptions are not our beliefs about something, although we will soon see how the two are related. Specifically, we will be looking at Gestalt ideas about seeing the big picture. Gestalt ideas about visual illusions date from about 1930 and encompass five main examples that we will examine in more detail.

We perceive the world of 3.5 dimensions—our perception of time in only one direction is the half. As we learn from Edwin Abbott Abbott's book *Flatland*, to perceive $n$ dimensions, a perceiver must exist in $n+1$ dimensions. Thus, humans exist in the 4.5[th] dimension. What would a being higher than us be able to do? Well, they could travel in time, and they could read the mental states of others (because our consciousness exists at the highest part of the 4.5$^{th}$ dimension). Thus, time travel and telepathy are favorite devices of the science-fiction author. Most of us cannot imagine further than that, though some physicists talk about eight or more dimensions.

So far, we have examined shapes that help us see the world in new ways—to empathize with others, make different choices, and connect more deeply with people. Now we examine some common mistakes we make with shapes. We have all read about cognitive biases and how we regularly err when making statistical guesses. This chapter looks at what I call "perceptual biases." We make mistakes in our perceptions of the world. Specifically, we use our sense perceptions and bring certain *appearances* into our personal philosophy or thinking.

Put slightly differently, our perceptions are not wrong, rather they *shape* the world we see. For example, the world usually looks flat when we walk around. Perceptions are the very first contact we have with the outer world. They translate the raw data outside of us into intelligible forms that we can think and act upon. Only after we have perceived something can we have thoughts or feelings about it. Our perceptions color the way we think. We all possess perceptual biases as part of our evolutionary heritage, not to mention various cultural biases.

Some common biases we have are illusions of control, illusions of certainty, and desires for closure. The fundamental nature of perception is quite alien to us because we take it for granted—so much so that we rarely notice our sense perceptions at work. For example, we smell something and recognize immediately what it is. We touch something and know it's smooth or prickly. We don't think about the complicated translation from raw input into judgments. We often assume that what we perceive through our senses is true. However, this is not the case. Thus, I review these sense perceptions because they are difficult to understand and too easy for us to trust.

*What are the main perceptual biases?*

Psychologists Daniel Kahneman and Amos Tversky outline several cognitive biases, and you can discover a few hundred more through an internet search. For example, the overconfidence bias says we tend to overrate our certainty versus actual probability calculations. The recency bias says we are apt to think something recent is more likely to happen again than something that happened long ago. The primacy bias is similar to a first impression: our first impressions of people have an inertia that persists despite changing data that prove us wrong. These cognitive biases are mistakes in our thinking. Once we become aware of them, we can attempt to correct them.

The perceptual biases grow out of research in Gestalt principles of visual perception. "Gestalt" is a German noun meaning "worldview," but you can also think of it as a holistic view, an amalgam, a big-picture orientation, or an overall sense of something. Dictionary.com defines it as "an organized whole that is perceived as more than the sum of its parts." Notice the word "perceived" in this definition. The organized whole is not necessarily more than its parts—it is only perceived that way.

*Figure and ground*

The main Gestalt principles we will study are: similarity, continuation, closure, proximity, and figure/ground. You may remember our discussion of foreground/background from an earlier chapter. The figure/ground idea is the same. It means that we immediately designate something we look at as a focal point, and the rest of our vision provides the background. There are a few optical illusions that tease us by switching back and forth, but for the most part, we always foreground one thing and background another.

*What is similarity?*

The "similarity principle" means that we tend to group similar things together. Have you ever separated M&Ms into different groups by color? Such groupings are very basic to humans. We separate people based on color and gender; later we advance to distinguishing them by beliefs or credentials. The real world is a jumble, but we organize it when possible so that it is easier for us to understand. For example, once we have separated the M&Ms, we can count them and compare how many there are of each color. It would be much harder to count them if we left them in a bowl and did not organize them. "Similarity" also refers to a big-picture view of things. If the night sky is dark except for five bright stars, we will naturally discern a shape or constellation from them. Clouds in the sky remind us of shapes we see on the ground.

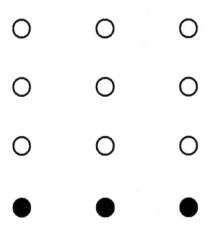

The counter-implication of this principle is that unlike or dissimilar things catch our attention. If all our M&Ms are red except for a blue one, our attention focuses immediately on the blue. Is the blue M&M more important than the red? Is it dangerous to the red M&Ms? Is it the leader of the M&Ms, or is it an outcast? While organizing things in this way is natural for us, we should not take it for the truth of how things exist in nature. This is obvious for stars and clouds and M&Ms, but we should especially keep this in mind when dealing with other people.

*What is continuation?*

Continuation deals with how we recognize certain shapes out of chaos. When we write an X, for example, we usually draw two straight lines that cross one another in the middle. If we see someone else's X or an X in nature, we may assume that it was drawn similarly. However, this is an assumption. Perhaps the X is a > right next to a < with the points touching. Or perhaps *four* straight lines created the X.

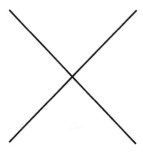

"Continuation" also refers to patterns that are more complicated, such as the individual human being. Within seven years, every cell in our bodies has changed, yet we see ourselves as the same person. In the morning we might wake up in the void, but soon our remembrance of who we are returns to us. We own certain things, we have certain obligations, and we have friends who seem to know us. As with the other perceptual biases, we often dislike the opposite concept. Here the opposite of continuation is change. Change presents a huge problem for most of us.

*What is closure?*

"Closure" is a crucial principle that greatly influences our personal philosophies. If you only remember one Gestalt principle, this is the one. We seek closure everywhere. From art, to shapes, to stories, to life itself, we want closure. We watch police dramas and we want the crooks to get captured. Not only do we hope for closure when we view certain shapes, we bring the same idea to our psychological wounds and traumas. The idea of closure can lead us astray, however, as life tends to be more complicated than that. Even when we die, our ideas and children live on.

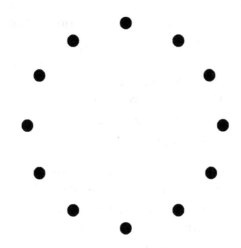

Visually speaking, our brains like to complete pictures. Impressionism or newsprint photographs made of dots automatically convert in our minds to their real-life counterparts. Thus, for example, when we see dots configured in a circular pattern, we automatically recognize a circle, even though the circle is not technically *there*. We may assume the artist meant to draw a circle, but even in natural landscapes, we like to complete our pictures with mental concepts by association.

More importantly, we like artistic forms to possess closure. Newspaper articles, short stories, novels, and movies are almost universally closed-form, rather than open-ended. When a story ends with a question, something nags at us as an audience. Often it is purposeful, to get the audience to imagine their own ending, or to provoke discussion, which then serves as the second half of the story.

Likewise, we do not like the world around us to resist closure. We want our wounds to heal—both physical and mental. Though we will keep our scars, we want justice from wrongs, and we want acclaim from rights. When we finally die, we want it to matter—somehow, somewhere. We want there to be a final accounting for good and bad, and we want the story of our individual lives to end with proper closure.

This desire for closure is very strong, but be aware that a desire is not the same as a truth. There might be closure in this world and there might not. Surely it is folly to assume that you always get what you want on Earth, but perhaps such thinking becomes the driving creative force that builds civilizations. Here I would simply stress awareness of our tendencies rather than a judgment of them.

*What is proximity?*

Finally, proximity is the principle of grouping things by their nearness to one another. The entire nation-state epoch rests upon the idea of contiguous proximity. Managing a country is much easier when all the land lies within a single closed loop. Borders become important and are much easier to define and defend. A few exceptions exist, such as Alaska for the United States or Kaliningrad for Russia. Of course, since September 11 and other times in history, the lines become blurry. We now live in a world where multinational corporations and organizations wield considerable power. The internet has also made location far less important. Thus, remember that while proximity means *something*, do not regard it as anything more than the starting point for further analysis.

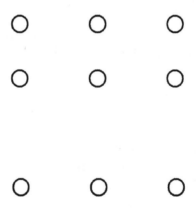

*Are there any other Gestalt perceptions?*

Additional Gestalt perceptions tend to be combinations of the basic ones outlined above. One unofficial and special case of this is called "pareidolia." This is exemplified in the tendency to see faces wherever we see two dots above another dot—a nose—or two dots above a horizontal line—a mouth. We are hardwired from birth, perhaps sooner, to recognize other human faces; after all, we are social creatures. Most of our attention and interest focuses on other humans. While we love certain pet animals, we rarely feel embarrassed or ashamed in front of them.

When the tendency to see faces activates, we see them everywhere. This is yet another case where we find that for which we search. In addition to seeing faces in various objects, animate or not, we imbue expressions: a surprised face, a happy face, a smug face. The point is that the human brain likes to make order out of randomness. But our thinking must not follow suit in seeing this order when it is not actually there. When we curtail these biases, our thinking will improve to become more objective, or less human-centered. This is a skill worth acquiring because we do not deal exclusively with humans. We also live in a world of nature.


*Conclusion*

We seek many other overarching patterns in the world; sometimes we find them, and sometimes we create them. For example, we seek symmetry, equality, and sometimes even *wabi sabi*. If we think of ourselves as the main characters in our own stories—and we do often think this—then the views of other people all become outsider perspectives. These are valuable to examine for myriad reasons, chiefly that we want to get along with other people. In addition, we add significantly more information to our own worldview by examining what others see that we either cannot or do not.

We are of course blind to our many flaws in part because our eyes look outward. We also inevitably live in a world of projection, where we assume either that other people are less important than we are or that they think in a fashion very similar to us. Humans all think similarly, yet we all think differently. We are all equals, yet we are not equal at all. These statements seem paradoxical on a general level, but that's because they're abstractions. When we add further detail, they become less abstract, and we find they are no longer paradoxical.

*Key Ideas*

- Perceptual biases are like visual illusions that we often mistakenly import into our thinking.

- There are five main Gestalt perceptions: continuity, similarity, proximity, closure, and figure/ground.

- The human brain likes to make order out of chaos.

*Discussion Questions*

- What additional Gestalt perceptual biases can you think of?

- In what kinds of cases are our perceptions closer to reality?

# chapter
# eleven

## Frameworks – Let's Borrow the Emperor's New Spectacles

*Overview*

A framework is the lens we use both to observe and solve a particular problem. For example, if you are a politician, you might see problems in terms of interest groups: groups with varying interesting vying to enact a single policy. A framework designates the particular inputs and outcomes you examine when making decisions.

Because the world is uncertain, it often pays to be a flexible thinker. In addition to rating the level of certainty we have about our various opinions and beliefs, we can also move back and forth between multiple frameworks. Flexible thinking allows us to realize multiple truths *at the same time*. In this chapter, we zoom our attention out to see the big picture from different vantage points. In the next chapter, we will learn how to zoom back in to see a more detailed problem from the point of view of another person.

Critical thinking is an important aspect of wisdom. We cannot simply follow mainstream attitudes and expect wisdom. We must find our own answers. One way to do this is through flexible thinking. Flexible thinking is the ability to use multiple frameworks for looking at the world. While we go through various examples, the ultimate goal is the ability to shuttle between these different frames at will. This gets our locus of conscious attention unstuck from its normal default state. We first turn to look at the morality lens through which we can view anything. After that, we look at binary options like optimism and pessimism.

## The Morality Lens

We tend to think in black and white when it comes to morality, but it would be more sophisticated to envision a spectrum. Killing a person is not equivalent to lying—or even bullying. And positive morality—doing the best that we ethically can with our time—also comes in many shapes and sizes. When we understand that there exists unlimited suffering in the world—and that humans possess only limited time—we begin to understand that every action we take or do not take contains a moral dimension—especially when we realize that morality includes doing good rather than simply avoiding harm. If you are looking for your purpose, I can tell you quite clearly now: your purpose is to help others. The idea of service seems to be quietly dying. But it is only when humans cooperate that we prove to the universe that we are growing up and becoming responsible caretakers. Instead of playing the role of the child who always needs more, we can become the adult who takes responsibility. We can be remarkable when we stand upon the shoulders of others. Whether these others came before us, or stand alongside us now, they represent untapped potential to help us with all the things we encounter on a daily basis that we know nothing about. Many organizations exist solely to make money, but there are so many additional types of organization that we could create. With our increasing isolation, we should probably replace dying shopping malls with various social group activities that we can implement ourselves.

## Frameworks

Sometimes called a paradigm, a framework is the lens through which we look at reality. Often this lens is the one we grow up with; it never changes and remains largely unexamined. Our framework represents all the assumptions we make about life—and unless we uncover these assumptions in some way, we live our entire lives in a kind of set illusion.

When a framework assumes everyone pursues his or her own self-interest, for example, our explanations for every behavior will be understood in these terms. For a hammer, everything becomes a nail. For a crowbar, every problem includes a crow. Sometimes in life we experience a paradigm shift, and everything we thought we knew becomes very clearly outmoded or wrong. This can happen by accident, or it can

193

happen through intentional critical thinking due to outside impetus. Now that we all have smart phones, for example, communication is quite different than it used to be. We must change our assumptions and ideas about communication when either new technologies or new problems arise.

In Chapter 4, we discussed dialectical thinking where two opposing viewpoints were simultaneously true. For example, most of us want connection and belonging in addition to independence. Some things can be true and false at the same time, depending upon how you look at them. Sometimes there are not only two opposing poles, but an infinite number of perspectives.

*Our beliefs*

Belief is a funny word in English. It usually denotes something that we do not know, yet act as if we know. For example, "I believe in God" can mean either I *want* to believe in god or I *know* there is a god. Actual knowledge should probably not use the word belief, yet our knowledge and beliefs can both be wrong. This chapter shows us a few ways that knowledge can be wrong—or at least incomplete. Of course, none of our *own* knowledge is wrong, but we can use this information to point out how our friends might be incorrect.

Some of our beliefs should be airy—especially when they are not particularly important to our identities. Some beliefs are far removed from our own knowledge and expertise, and we might consider treating them as such. We do not need to have opinions on every geopolitical topic, even though as Americans we are taught how every voice counts in an election. Democracy is a good framework for some decisions, but not *every* decision.

### The problem with having only one framework

A common social debate centers around how much our lives are based on nature versus nurture. I would venture that nature, nurture, randomness, and spirit are all important factors in our lives. But if you want to argue the nature framework, for example, you might focus first upon genes or DNA. The point of life in this framework is to pass on our DNA and genes. Thus, humans are just passenger busses that are far less important than the cargo we carry of genes and DNA. DNA 'wants' to replicate and a gene 'wants' to live on in the next generation. Ironically, such a framework that explains everything soon explains nothing. And indeed, few people mention this framework nowadays. We do not want to rob ourselves of our own power, or agency, in life. Sure, there are things outside our control, but not everything is.

Similarly, if someone believes that everything that happens is God's will, they do not leave much room for human creativity, power, sins, aspirations, or even fun. In fact, we might agree that everything is God's will, then quickly move on to the second question of why we should do anything at all. In other words, when we look for a *good* explanation, we actually look for something that is only *partly* explanatory. We don't want God or genes to explain *everything*. We want a system that gives us an opening where our choices can matter too. We want neither pure order nor pure chaos, but something between these two extremes. And that is what we find. Similarly, not everything should be about money. If someone truly thinks this, they become a distorted and shallow person. Finally, not everything should be about "me"—whoever the me is. When a person assumes everything in the world somehow revolves around him or her, they have extreme narcissism. At best this skews their understanding and at worst makes them intolerable for the rest of us.

*Mindfulness and changing frameworks*

Many spiritual teachers these days promote mindfulness. Mindfulness is when we pay close attention to the present moment. We eat our food slowly and taste every nuance. Or we listen intently to another person's story.

How does using a framework compare to practicing mindfulness? I would say they are opposites, yet as we learned in Chapter 3 and again in Chapter 7, this makes them two sides of the same coin. We can alternate our conscious attention between being mindfulness and the trying out of various frameworks. Likewise, we can choose a framework either before or after we find a problem.

According to Ellen Langer, mindfulness happens in the absence of a mindset. A mindset is simply what we are calling a framework. Mindfulness is attending to life—showing up, in other words. But what is a *mindset*? A mindset conjures the idea of a set plan—a script. Remember from Chapter 1, when we live life from a script, we are not cultivating real connection. Mindfulness, then, is like *improvisation*, while a mindset is a *set* framework.

The ability to switch mindsets at will is perhaps the pinnacle of cognitive empathy and wisdom, and *contrasts* with: a life lived fully in flow, a life in tune with the Tao, the meditative state of no-mind, or Tolle's state of stillness and presence in the now. As we usually understand it, wisdom is reserved for those times when we are reflective, rather than living in flow. Perfect knowledge is not the same as wisdom. An omniscient god is not *wise*. Wisdom is the practical method that *humans* use to deal with uncertainty.

In sum, then, we all possess at least one worldview by default. The *aha* moment comes when we realize that we can choose and change our worldviews. (If you are blind, you have probably been waiting this whole book for an acknowledgement, and I provide that now. I habitually scan text for bias—which is ever-present— and the word understanding is almost always used with eyeball metaphors.)

*How might we first encounter new frameworks?*

Many people operate within a single framework for their entire lives. How can we first crack open this kind of mind to realize the magic of using multiple frameworks? Studying philosophy and critical thinking are direct paths to gain the meta-awareness necessary to shuffle between frameworks. Perhaps the next best intentional gateway for encountering a new framework is to learn a new language. Beginning language classes for adults are usually a lot fun as well. When we learn a new language, we realize that words are elastic concepts. Since a lot of our thoughts are words, we learn a new perspective on our thoughts. Learning a new language also opens the doors to new cultures that are different from our own. While a language itself might seem superficial, the cultural insight and realization of different vantage points make it a profound learning experience.

Of course, the unintentional gateway for seeing multiple frameworks is growing up as a minority in a society where the mainstream framework differs from the minority framework. There is usually a mainstream culture that everyone knows, then there are subcultures that only group members fully understand. From an early age, then, one sees the world from two perspectives—what W.E.B. Dubois called *double consciousness*. While we can transcend our personal identities under certain circumstances, society also places identities upon us like a two-way street, like a dialectic. These can be difficult or impossible to completely escape.

We are inundated with the mainstream perspective, although we can choose to learn more about subcultures and cultural outsiders that think and act differently from this. When we respect these other people, we acknowledge that there are indeed multiple perspectives upon the same world. We are all minorities in some aspect, but of course the deeper this aspect of our identity goes, the more we might learn versatility in choosing our frameworks.

*What are some examples of frameworks?*

The easiest frameworks to discuss are *binary* frameworks. Here we have a choice of looking at the world from one perspective or the other. For example, the most well-known frameworks are *optimism* versus *pessimism*. The optimist looks at the good side of life, while the pessimist looks at the same world, but sees it in a negative light.

Identification as a Republican or a Democrat is another common dichotomy. No independently thinking person would support a full party platform because this is simply a statistical mishmash to garner 50% of the votes. That is, interest groups and coalitions form to reach a majority and agree to vote *with* one another. Politicians do not actually agree with any entire platform, so why should you? When you see a 'surrogate' on television who toes the party line in everything, you can see they are not being thoughtful—they are getting paid to parrot. In my opinion, only actual politicians or unaligned thinkers should be given such a wide venue to speak. Otherwise, we get division and talking points instead of insight.

We also face a framework, or personal philosophy, when voting. Consider the following scenario: you agree with 10% of the Democratic platform, 20% of the Republican platform, and 50% of a third-party platform. Who do you vote for? The answer depends upon your framework. Are you practical or idealistic? Should you vote for someone who can win or should you vote your conscience? What if, by voting for the third-party candidate, the person you agree with the *least* ends up winning?

Compromising is difficult, and the more principled we become the more difficult it is. However, the *perfect* is often the enemy of the good enough. Seeing multiple frameworks allows us to compromise when a decision is important. There are also times to remain principled, and some principles are clearly worth dying for. Just be sure these principles are of utmost importance to you. Socrates, Buddha, Jesus and others had certain principles worth dying for, so principles are not anathema to wisdom. But remember that you can change your life today if you simply change your mind.

It is also important to remember: frameworks are *all* limiting beliefs. The ability to choose a *new* framework is what gives us power. If we can truly see several truths at once, we become a lot *less* limited. But just as we saw early on in Chapter 2, to foreground one thing is always to background another. Foregrounding multiple ideas in succession is like seeing multiple frameworks in succession, and this is as close as we can get to wide understanding.

In spirituality, we hear a lot about abundance versus scarcity mindsets. Often, we are taught to believe in the scarcity mindset, while the mystic tends toward an abundance mindset. A more updated version of this are the growth versus fixed mindsets, or even love versus fear mindsets. A fixed mindset is the inability to think flexibly, while a growth mindset is an open and brave attitude toward new ideas. Growth lies in the realization that we can choose a new way of looking at the world. Indeed, we can choose *many* ways. We can ask new questions, look at background information in a new way, or choose to see the world from someone else's viewpoint.

*The mystic's framework*

The mystic's job is to invert our common-sense assumptions about the world and pan for gold in the form of useful ideas. We have touched upon these ideas throughout the book, but we recall them now. For example, wisdom takes time and experience, but Eckhart Tolle finds wisdom without the need for more time. The power is in the present moment.

Also, we can invert subject and object: do we play the game, or does the game play us? Do we own our possessions, or do they own us? We can invert cause and effect: are we humans having a spiritual experience, or are we spirits having a human experience? Do victimizers enjoy wielding power, or are they enacting a learned behavior that keeps them stuck in a victim mentality of their own? Indeed, in an attempt to mimic the mystic, we can create a new 'false' or inverse belief and follow where it leads us. Science fiction and comic books sometimes show this kind of mirror world.

*Repurposing the usual tools at our disposal: eyes, cameras, and maps*

As a more detailed metaphor for understanding, we can imagine that our thoughts work like our eyes. We focus our laser eyes upon a specified area within our environment. By default, this is a horizontal oval, but we can choose a new size and shape for our imaginary focus area.

A camera also has an aperture and a lens. We look at a snapshot for any instant in time, or we can see the world as a moving, evolving process. We can

201

distort an image with a fisheye lens. A camera has an aperture that lets light in for a specified amount of time. In theory, this aperture can be any shape and stay open as long as desired.

One final example: maps are often generated to emphasize accurate geography. But instead of this emphasis, we can look at the world through a *population* map where the countries are sized based on their populations rather than square miles. Imagine all the different ways we could emphasize new perspectives by changing our frameworks like this.

*Key Ideas*

- Flexible thinking allows us to see multiple truths at the same time

- Every decision we make or do not make contains a moral component

- Mindfulness is the absence of a mindset

- Shuffling through multiple mindsets is a way to see multiple truths

- Learning philosophy or a second language are intentional gateways to see multiple frameworks

- The mystic inverts common sense assumptions to discover or relate an important truth


*Discussion Questions*

- What additional mindsets can we use to look at the world? Are they all binary?

- What could world maps emphasize besides population or geographic accuracy?

- What are some common assumptions you can invert, or turn sideways?

# chapter twelve

## Angles of Perception – Relationships – Sensory Awareness

*Overview*

You may have noticed that this book does not contain many stories. Personally, I do not like stories because they add weight to one's identity. I like to take myself more lightly. But most people love stories. Indeed, stories or narratives are important in communication. Specifically, they tie us to mythical archetypes and they give our identities greater significance. However, the stories we tell ourselves are also quite changeable. When we tell a different story about ourselves, we have changed our identity to some extent. Perhaps this is why I distrust stories. Aside from this caveat, stories are great ways to learn from other people's perspectives. We have much to learn from people who have different life experiences. In Chapter 7, we discussed expanding the circle of our ingroup to encompass more and more people. Here we briefly discuss how to access these new viewpoints. First, we look at the idea of multiple perspectives. Second, we look at feminist critiques of mainstream values by focusing on the idea of relatedness. Third, we look at sensory awareness as a rarely used pathway toward development.

*Multiple Perspectives*

The main understanding of empathy is the ability to walk a mile in another person's shoes—or moccasins. While we might agree with this notion, there are few well-known methods to help us enact this practice. The exceptions that I know of are method acting and reading literature.

How else can we move our center of consciousness—our locus of being—into the body of another person or thing? A central component of human social cognition is the ability to attribute mental states to ourselves and others. This ability is often referred to as 'mentalizing' or 'theory of mind'. The opposite of the recognition that other people have minds of their own is called solipsism. Sometimes the pathway to growth is first realizing other people exist, and then learning how to get along with them.

Without stories, how do we connect to different perspectives? Well, we could try becoming more aware of our vision; things actually *look* different to different people. Are other people simply wrong? Let me present an example. What does the following shape look like to you?

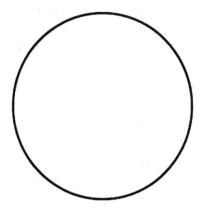

If you hold your book or device directly in front of you, this is a circle. However, if you lay down the book and ask the person at the table sitting across from you what shape it is, they will see an oval. Their minds could correct for their perspective, and they might know it is actually a circle, but from a 45-degree angle, this circle appears as an oval. You can try this game on your own by setting up mirrors and finding an asymmetric object. This object will appear differently depending upon where you view it—in the mirror or as you rotate it.

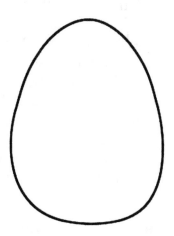

The world of ideas and social interaction are no different. What you see is merely a single perspective. You can communicate with others to discover the particular aspects that are hidden to you. Most of us cannot envision an asymmetric object in our heads—we must mentally rotate it to see the back. If you don't believe me, try envisioning the planet Earth and the location of various continents without mentally *moving* the globe inside your head. This straightforward task is beyond most of us—we tend to see things as flat. (I do not know whether this is hard-wired or merely cultural.)

How else can we use this knowledge of multiple perspectives? We can reflect upon our own ideas. We can turn ourselves into the "other" in order to see ourselves in a new light. This allows us to step back and see new facets of ourselves that we usually do not see. If you have a trusted friend, you might ask them to help you with this task. Again, you can use mirrors, but there are some visions of ourselves that should remain unknown to us.

Ultimately, we can practice this *spatial shifting* in more original ways. Examine an event like the 2007 financial crisis or the 2016 election. Examine how this event would appear from the perspectives of different people—Republicans, Democrats, Bernie Sanders, independents, or various interest groups. The world looks different to these different groups. I am not saying there is not some objective reality out there—I *am* saying that such a reality is beside the point. We do not live within an objective reality but in a socially and scientifically limited piece of it.

We now turn to one specific critique of the dominant paradigm. We take a moment to imagine a feminine approach to culture. Remember from Chapter 3 that feminine does not mean a generalization like all women. It is simply a way to describe one end of a spectrum of ideas.

*Feminist Critiques of Development*

Psychologist Carol Gilligan is a researcher who writes about the disenfranchisement of women both in the field of psychology and in actual psychological theories. An individuated or self-actualized "self" is often upheld as the ultimate end-point in development, but this is a masculine ideal. Following from yin-yang ideas, other typically "masculine" qualities include control, rationality, abstract principle-driven ethics, detachment, and independence. Certain opposing "feminine" qualities include authenticity, empathy, and the drive to connect. (Robb, 2006, p. x) Psychological theories—and indeed our culture—tend to rate the masculine qualities as more important and higher value.

Like the Gestalt concept of continuity from Chapter 10, the concept of *consistency* is also held up as an important virtue. Consistency is part of principle-based logic and is another prized goal of many theorists, though there is rarely justification for why consistency is either good or more helpful than inconsistency. Of course, the context of how and where we are consistent is also important. In short, we often value consistency, but rarely prove that it is important. We just accept it like a fundamental yet hidden assumption of our theories.

*Relationships*

Just as in the idea of horizontal spirituality from Chapter 7, we can choose relationships as the locus of our attention—we do not need to analyze everything from the perspective of the individual person. Ruthellen Josselson argues this point in *The Space Between Us* from 1996. Similar to network analysis, Josselson asks her subjects to draw diagrams of circles representing people and lines representing the connections between them—thus graphically depicting the key relationships in people's lives. Unlike network analysis, however, she focuses not on the *nodes* as the unit of interest, but on the *lines*. People do not exist in isolation, rather it is their relationships that define reality and in fact *compose* reality. "We know ourselves as separate only insofar as we live in connection with others." (Gilligan 1982, p. 63)

And in line with the themes behind green spirituality, Josselson suggests, "Devaluation of relatedness is another form of destroying our environment: we trample on that which constitutes our world." In her book, she presents eight different types of relatedness, ranging from attachment to care-giving. They involve "a way of transcending space, of reaching through space (or being reached) and being in contact with each other." In sum, relatedness has been devalued by our culture, even while it is the arena where we experience our most meaningful moments. Developing our relationships more fully is an analogous but different pathway than that of self-development.


*Sensory Awareness*

In addition to moving our locus of attention to other people, things, and relationships, Charlotte Selver reminds us to turn our attention to the awareness of our senses. When we come to a standing position, "do we *stand on our own feet*, as we have so often been exhorted to, or do we stand *on the floor*?" Sensory awareness gives us new avenues to explore the world, and we often feel more connected to the world when we focus our attention on our sensory perceptions.

Sensory awareness is a subject for experience rather than thinking. We have at least five senses. Bringing attention to our various sensations connects us to the world outside our heads. More practice in this realm creates the possibility to pro-act rather than re-act to our many perceptions.

*Key Ideas*

- Stories are often how we learn about different life experiences.

- Method acting and literature teach us how to see the world from different perspectives.

- Shapes, the world itself, and even ourselves all look different from different angles.

- Mainstream development theories often focus on the self, but relationships also develop.

- We can focus our attention upon the space between us instead of ourselves.

- Sensory awareness grounds us to the Earth and is an often overlook place to focus our consciousness.

*Discussion Questions*

- How can we make learning from other people's stories more systematic?

- What are some things that you have learned about other people from literature or acting?

- How do relationships develop, and what would be their potential zenith?

- How could we talk about ourselves only in terms of relationship?

- How many senses do you possess? I think there are many more than five. Are all your senses equally well-developed?

# chapter
# thirteen

*The Blueprint Chapter –*
*Construct Your Own Shape*

*"Take my advice for I am an old man: never take advice."*

– Jose Ortega y Gasset

*"Independence is happiness."*

– Susan B. Anthony

*Overview*

The first quote above is of course paradoxical. Should we take this advice or not? Similarly, I have tried to present you with options to investigate further rather than a set of rules. We all have our personal truths, especially when it comes to our emotions. Use what resonates for *you*. No stranger can deny your feelings. Yes, if our opinions are largely unpopular, we might run into difficulty. We thus walk a tightrope between individual power and social power. Perhaps we can transcend our personal identities but cannot transcend our social identities. Other people do matter, especially when they hold power over us. We are formed through multiple interlinking systems. This final chapter exhorts you to take as much personal power as you can, while recognizing the power of others to shape you.

## Spiritual Independence and Transformative Creativity

One main underlying theme of this book is that we must be individuals who are community-minded. To live the best life, we treat ourselves and others as equal in importance. Because we do possess power as individuals, we must attend to the groups we join, the company we keep, and the ideas we send out into the world. It is expected that different people will have different opinions, but we are not our opinions—we are much more. We are complicated creatures and thus beautiful. Go out and say hello to *people*—not their opinions.

While a mediocre education teaches you *what* to think, a good education teaches you *how* to think. Perhaps a great education teaches you how to think *independently*. Education is a gradual process from exposure to internalization. A teacher presents us with new information. We study until we can replicate this knowledge. Eventually we become self-sufficient in the subject and no longer need the teacher. We have internalized certain principles that allow us to seek any further answers on our own. A successful and complete education thus ends with a transformation: upon subject mastery, the pupil becomes the teacher. When the original teachers are secure individuals, they will take pride as their pupil eventually surpasses them.

In the preceding chapters, we employed various shapes to help us examine the world with fresh eyes. I chose these particular shapes because they were informative, commonplace, or both. But the ultimate goal of this education is not for you to merely memorize *my* shapes, but to begin building your own. With your change from passive observer to active participant, you will move from *understanding* the world toward *creating* the world.

By constructing our own shapes, we begin to construct our own *lives*. The capstone project to graduate from this thinking course is to create a new shape, then share it with the public on a website. This chapter will guide you through the process. Our goal is to simplify the world yet not to take our shapes too seriously. We want to enhance our creativity—not rigidly adhere to some kind of absolute truth. As a scientist would caution, let the data tell the story—do not make up a theory and then look for supporting data.

Jiddu Krishnamurti was a famous Indian spiritual teacher. For years the Theosophical Organization built up around his teachings. But when he finally took the helm of the organization, he dissolved it—in effect telling his followers that they must seek their own truths through introspection. He says, "I maintain that truth is a pathless land, and you cannot approach it by any path whatsoever, by any religion, by any sect... I desire to free men from all cages, from all fears, and not to found religions, new sects, nor to establish new theories and new philosophies." Like Epicurus, Krishnamurti felt that psychological courage was the only path toward human progress.

*Your first shape*

When we hear the word 'creative' we envision painters, composers, or writers—people that work in the creative arts. But creativity is not just about painting or writing stories. We are *all* expert creators: we create our very lives, from the identities we cling to, to the stories we tell ourselves about who we really are. One might respond that we inherit many of our qualities, and this is true, but how we choose to think about and use these qualities is often under our control. Education is liberating not because it increases our options in the workplace, but because it teaches us about other people's decisions—it increases our awareness about how much in life is actually subject to direct control.

Socrates famously asked questions more often than he provided answers. He sought truth through logical discourse. Other teachers use introspective approaches like meditation. In the realm of human beings, truth is often context dependent. Your personal truth may be that you like strawberries, but that doesn't imply that strawberries are good in any objective or societal sense. For many important questions in your life, you must rely on your own logic and taste. Personal logic is not always open to easy communication. When we know certain things to be true that we are not able to communicate to others, we begin to enter the dimension of spirituality. Free yourself, that you may free others.

To construct your first shape, remember that you can divide anything into two pieces. We can invert subject and object, or we can simply move around our locus of attention by taking on multiple perspectives. We decompose our theories into the tiniest bits we can manage. One size does not fit all, thus we bring in factor analysis. Factor analysis is a statistical tool that helps us focus on how various parts of a phenomenon gather into segments or factions. For example, we might find that most people in our study like only two out of an infinite number of colors. Thus, these two colors become our two factors. This practice helps you theorize, but more importantly it teaches us how models become limited and never fully true. Feel free to share your theory with someone else and watch them pick it to pieces. This work of pattern matching and then getting feedback from others is the basic learning process of humanity. My hope is that you now see that the simpler the model you create, the less truth and importance it holds.

This book remains unfinished until you, the reader, put something from it into practice to improve your life or the world. Thank you for reading. While not an expert wordsmith, I hoped to offer you a lot of new ideas. Our culture's grand narratives are not particularly numerous these days. If you found any useful ideas here, please review the book somewhere online to help others find it. You are also free to dispute anything I write here either publicly or privately. Most importantly, take some time to reconsider your life, then charge ahead and go live it.

*Final thoughts*

If I could advise one authoritarian project for the United States, I would create one shared framework as a ritual of passage to adulthood. I think we would personally and nationally benefit by requiring one year of national service for teenagers after high school. This would provide real-life belonging rather than mere myths about America's identity. Of course, I would also require a class in wisdom while there—to teach the limits of patriotism and the value of multiple frameworks. We would have a capstone 'thinking course' to debrief us on what all our learning was about. Teenagers would naturally groan about these requirements, then they would fondly remember their experiences for the rest of their lives. Such a national requirement would provide the bi-directional benefits of service—to the givers and to the receivers.

Young people would get paid to learn teamwork skills and to learn firsthand how diverse skills and viewpoints improve decisions rather than simply cause snags. Good teamwork can be a very inspirational experience. It can be so much more than simply worrying that your lab partner will shirk his or her duties to your shared school project. When we cooperate, we can create unimaginable things.

Many college graduates look back at dormitory life as their happiest years. Learning and living as equals are enjoyable life choices, yet after college we are all told to move in the opposite direction—toward isolation, an end to learning, and hierarchy chasing. Adam Smith was a strong proponent of cooperation and charity and would be appalled at the claims made in his name by many free market champions of today. The real world can be what we make it. It does not have to be about bullying and competition. It can be about enjoyable cooperation with make-believe rivalries—like games, or as some call it, *co-opetition*.

Let me offer a final piece of advice. When I was young, I thought I would become a wealthy and lonely man. I was wrong on both counts. Always choose love over money. You become the beacon by shining your light onto everyone else. This focus on others is your greatest purpose, and when you share your light, it gets brighter and brighter. This is how you spread enlightenment. This is why the gods punished Prometheus when he brought humans fire. They realized that with teamwork and cooperation, the sky was the limit for humanity.

If you found value in this book, please review it somewhere online to help other people find it. If you did not like it, I also welcome negative feedback. In any case, I humbly and heartily thank you for reading!

# t h e   e n d

the end

# a p p e n d i x
# a

## *Wisdom and Decision-Making*

*Overview*

Let's imagine an old man or woman watching young children playing. The children have an argument. To the old ones, this is a game. They chuckle. This is how a sage or sagess looks upon *adults*—and the entire world. If these wise people were living 150 years ago, perhaps this would make sense. But today, sages do not have to live as long to gain wisdom. This means it is not all about age. There are things all of us can do to become wiser. Besides thinking creatively, we can *experience* more in the time we have. Rather than aiming for wisdom, however, I suggest we try to make wiser decisions. This piecemeal method follows an incremental approach to life, which is second only to living in the present moment.

This appendix explains how to make wiser decisions.

223

*Do we still need role models?*

Our society should no longer abide the notion of role models in our culture. Perhaps role models made sense when information was scarce, but this is no longer the case. First, role models have a nasty habit of disappointing people. Second, everyone brings their own voices and uniqueness to this world. Anyone who tells you otherwise is failing to see your light.

In this appendix, we will look at some of the wisest people in history. Yes, they had faults. We all have faults. We accept that, but it makes no sense to emulate that aspect of people—only to know that it will always be there.

What can we use in place of role-models? Traits and skills. Most traits are skills that we can learn about, practice, and improve. Wisdom is not a trait; what we call wise decision-making is a *skill*—a learnable skill. Even caring is a learnable skill. "Wisdom" is the name we give to a thought process that involves cognition, emotion, and reflection. We all can bring this kind of awareness into our decision-making.

*What is wisdom?*

Wisdom is knowing our place in the world. We are social animals—more social than sharks but less social than ants and bees. Wisdom is ethical and concerned with the bigger picture. The opposite of wisdom is often unethical behavior. Unethical behavior is not bad because it breaks rules; it is bad for the bad actors themselves. Philosopher Bertrand Russell warns us against such practices: "What are the really harmful acts to which the average man is tempted? Sharp practice in business of the sort not punished by law, harshness towards employees, cruelty towards wife and children, malevolence towards competitors, ferocity in political conflicts—these are the really harmful sins that are common among respectable and respected citizens." Sin is defined by Eastern philosopher Alan Watts as missing the point. Indeed, the person who behaves malevolently is not living an appropriate life—nor even a fulfilling one.

Wisdom is a type of deep *and* broad thinking. The earth we cling to hurtles through space as part of an ever-expanding universe. The truth is alive: it is dynamic, open-ended, and aware of its own reflection in the funhouse mirror. In short, we enjoy the perfect setting for limitless exploration. Wisdom is the gauge of our progress on this journey toward truth. It represents one idealized endpoint of human development.

Wisdom is interdisciplinary—indeed, trans-disciplinary—and thus there are as many definitions of it as there are specialized languages. Even worse, language is itself a poor substitute for truth. If a picture is worth a thousand words, a truth is worth a million. Wisdom is perhaps seeing a larger slice of truth. However, because truth is dynamic and open-ended, wisdom likewise contains a tacit factor that we can never fully codify. Since every context is different, and every person is unique, how could "wisdom" mean only one thing? The fine line we have walked in this book was therefore between a definition too vague and one too specific—the former making wisdom too simple, the latter making it too exclusive.

This book explored the topic of wisdom—that broadest of all human considerations—through stories, visuals, and exposition. Defined in bare-bones style, "wisdom" is the consistent ability to make intentional decisions in the face of uncertainty. The word "intentional" here separates wisdom from both instinct and certainty—times when wisdom is not required. Wise decisions need not be strictly rational, since we live with the effects of our emotions as surely as we live with the consequences of logic. However, a wise decision must consider cognitive and emotional biases, specifically the more common logical fallacies as well as mismatches between intuition and mathematical probability. Additionally, wise decisions differ from other decisions by the sets of inputs and outcomes that come under consideration. Describing these inputs and outcomes formed the main substance of this book.

*Where does one look for wisdom?*

To tackle the study of any topic, we first decide what unit of analysis to focus on. We know that wisdom follows from understanding; thus, we will cast our nets wide to search for ideas that are both imitable and useful. We will apply any insights to the individual human level, as most of us are in no position to alter a larger unit, either ethically or practically. The search for inputs to a wise decision will be limitless, the action point will be the single human decision, and the outcomes will again be limitless. For practical reasons, we limit our search to three main categories: patterns in nature, patterns in individual human behavior, and patterns in human group behavior. Of course, these domains overlap.

Wisdom is a distinctly human phenomenon. Birds will fly, dogs will bark, and humans will ponder, though there are exceptions to every rule. It is no accident that Plato considered philosophy—the search for truth, beauty, and wisdom—to be the apex of human activity. However, humans not only think, we engage with the world, as Aristotle's praxis reminds us. We also feel emotions—to the chagrin of ancient Greeks everywhere.

Because gods already possess certainty, they do not need wisdom. At the opposite end of the knowledge spectrum, our animal friends do not ponder various options at length before acting. However, while the nonhuman world has no need of wisdom, it exhibits patterns and phenomena that we would be wise to imitate. For example, the *Tao Te Ching* advises us that "The best man is like water. Water is good; it benefits all things and does not compete with them." For Taoists— and for all of us—the natural world will become our classroom. Although we can just as easily imagine the destructive impacts of water through hurricanes or tsunamis.

While aphorisms are appealing, wisdom is often context-dependent and therefore not as simple as stating aphorisms. Indeed, the *Tao Te Ching* begins by saying that words are a poor substitute for truth, and then proceeds with an entire book on the subject.

Nowadays we are more apt to take material from nature than philosophy, yet the natural world—through its vistas and biodiversity—nonetheless offers fertile ground for ideas. While ancient philosophers took this source for granted, centuries of urban migration have divorced us from what might now seem like primitive behavior. However, we can have our cake and eat it too: we can remain civilized while still learning from nature. Knowledge of natural processes helps us when we wish to work either with such patterns or against them: harness the wind but keep the air conditioner running. Indeed, scientists now look to bio-inspiration—studying biomimetic systems—with the goal of copying complex natural systems to solve human problems.

In addition to looking at nature, we of course looked at the relatively more familiar patterns of humans, both as individuals and in various-sized clusters. While the common definition of "culture" refers to a group's shared set of values and customs, here I distinguish culture from nature: culture represents the degree of artificiality of a human group. The more cultured a person is, then, the further his or her attitudes and behaviors will depart from the purely instinctual. While this supplement to the standard definition of "culture" implies that some groups will thereby possess *more* culture than others, it maintains a certain relativity of value judgments. A group with more culture is not necessarily a better or more progressive group; only one that is further from animal callings. This is not always a good thing. For example, killing a person for his belief system is a distinctly human phenomenon, however, such a practice in no way represents an *advance* from animal behavior.

Can a culture exhibit wisdom? If a wise culture survives, a yet wiser culture *thrives*. The wisest culture perfectly balances the needs of all of its diverse members, all while maintaining order and a relatively pleasant environment. Of course, when we speak in aggregates, the theory becomes simple because we have abstracted to the point of absurdity. Most of us cannot order our own minds, let alone an entire society.

*Role models in wisdom*

As individuals, we largely pattern our attitudes and behaviors after role models and cultural archetypes, including fictional characters and situations. As we turn our attention to the personal, our first task is to uncover human exemplars of wisdom. What characterizes a wise person? Does a wise person survive and thrive? Perhaps, though not necessarily.

Several years ago, I began hosting monthly wisdom workshops. Our first priority was to define wisdom. To this end, we nominated wise people—paragons of judiciousness—in an inductive approach to uncover common themes. The usual suspects appeared: Jesus, Socrates, Gandhi, Buddha, and Abraham Lincoln, to name a few. Except in the case of Buddha, one common denominator appeared to be death by assassination. (Do we commonly assassinate wise people, or do we posthumously bestow the mantle of wisdom upon those who have been thus wronged?) Additional critiques of these beacons of sagacity ensued. For example, Buddha abandoned his family; Gandhi's success in expelling the British led to a bloody civil war.

After considerable discussion, we found ourselves wary of proclaiming *anyone* undeniably wise. However, we did agree that our nominees made wise decisions within compartmentalized aspects of their lives. We also discussed the idea that, as corporeal beings, we all possessed a dark side, if for no other reason than the need to feed on other life to live. Our best course of action when faced with this dark side, Carl Jung suggests, is to acknowledge it rather than suppress it and feed it.

When we express a desire to change the world, and then actually begin the work needed to affect this change, we soon realize that our own language has deceived us. This is not one action at all, but rather a long series of minute actions that we must take. When aggregated—which is intensely easy with language—these microscopic actions add up to an individual life. These individual lives then add up to a society, and these societies add up to the world. The focus throughout this book has been on the level of the individual decision; indeed, here I introduce the concept of "person-moment" to convey how microscopically we must examine things in order to make any sense of them whatsoever. However, at the same time, we must never consider a thing to exist in true isolation.

One might ask: how can we call a decision wise before evaluating its outcome? Indeed, a single decision can alternate between being wise and unwise for years due to changing environments that are not even under our control, such as in this book's many examples. So, if the final judgment is perpetually yet to come, how can we boldly deem any decision wise? If we are to say anything useful, we must devise criteria for wise decisions that are independent of their outcomes. As previously mentioned, we label a decision "wise" when it contains certain input factors and certain *intended* outcomes.

We now take a brief detour to examine how wisdom might benefit a society, but not necessarily the person who pursues it.

*Why we need social wisdom: specialists and generalists*

When applying for a job, a candidate tailors his or her resume to the position, projecting the image that a person's whole life has been dedicated to getting this job—which is precisely what the hiring manager wants. (We are, of course, assuming a meritocracy here.) While some people do lead focused lives, most do not. For example, I possess an undergraduate degree and two graduate degrees, but all in different disciplines—in fact, the three areas that partition modern academia: sciences, social sciences, and humanities. Such broad knowledge hinders my job prospects, yet renders me among the more interesting conversationalists at a cocktail party. (I mean, would you rather listen to the entomologist who relates everything he hears back to bugs, or the person who takes the word "bugs" and associates it with cartoons, surveillance, minor annoyances, etc., then tells you the funniest story out of that lot? Actually—come to think of it—the entomologist who relates *everything* to bugs would be quite hilarious, at least for a few hours.) In any case, it pays to be a specialist, but people tend to prefer generalists outside of office hours.

While wisdom presents us with countermeasures against the dangers that accompany specialization and the eventual dislocations that arise when certain problematic attitudes remain unchecked, wisdom is not *en vogue*. Indeed, when specialization increasingly offers the individual greater *financial* success, the exploration of wisdom and big-picture thinking suffers corresponding neglect. Why would anyone pursue broad thinking under such a system?

The problems are not merely institutional. Would you rather the very best surgeon performed your operation, or would you settle for a satisfactory surgeon who also happens to be a violin virtuoso? Specialists are important, however not every problem requires surgery. In fact, most surgeons will tell you that the less invasive the solution, the better. Medicine is a field that has embraced the generalist/specialist dichotomy more than most. While healthcare is certainly expensive, it is also very noticeably advancing. In many fields, generalists remain underappreciated due to conflation with bureaucrats. Outside of fields altogether, generalists are even more critical, but who pays them and who listens to them?

It certainly compounds the problem when the very people who are most able to generalize shy away from specialization, to look on only as outsiders. Institutional exclusion combines with this self-selection process to create two separate worlds: the specialists who speak to others within their chosen field, and the exiles. I wrote this book for these exiles, but I hope that the specialists found something interesting here as well.

*Who needs wisdom?*

Wisdom can certainly help stabilize society, but

what rewards await the *individual* pursuing wisdom? Just as social wisdom involves uniting groups with different agendas, the wise person may experience a sense of personal integrity. The pathway to wisdom is not the same as the pathway to happiness, however, for we cannot preemptively restrict our learning to only discovering *happy* truths. To echo the sentiment expressed in the book of Ecclesiastes: with increased knowledge comes increased sorrow. By its very nature, wisdom is a calling—not a pursuit toward selfish ends. Indeed, it requires no vow of poverty, for that would be redundant.

Wisdom represents a goal for those willing to examine the world, themselves, and others without applause for their efforts. While wisdom does not promise acclaim, happiness, or wealth, author W.E.B. Du Bois reminds us that we never regret an education, as we receive something invaluable—though indescribable—from it. Though it may sadden our countenance, we never wish it undone. He explains this through a fictional John who is talking with an old friend: "John," she said, "does it make everyone—unhappy when they study and learn lots of things?" He paused and smiled. "I am afraid it does," he said. "And John, are you glad you studied?" "Yes," came the answer, slowly but positively.

Personally, I like to think of education as "climbing the unhappy mountain." Why climb this mountain? Why climb *any* mountain? Because it is there. And perhaps it presents a sublime view.

*What is a good life?*

A good life is not free of suffering, but it engenders a sort of satisfaction. In general, a good life requires commitment to one's personal needs, as well as service to others. While spirituality teaches us that these are two sides of the same coin, suffice it to say that making the world a better place improves conditions for everybody living in it—including you.

When did people start thinking about making the world a better place? The ideas of self-improvement and societal improvement date back to starry-eyed optimists since time immemorial. Thousands of years ago, Aristotle provided guidelines for living a good life. Unfortunately, the connotations of the word "good" have changed considerably over time. In today's world, something that is "good for you" is often unpleasant, at best. Another connotation of "good" implies the dichotomy of good versus evil: the "good life" is some sort of ethical code imposed upon us from outside—by society—to help us live in harmony. This connotation is better but still somewhat unpleasant, since the locus of control comes from outside. Finally—perhaps due to successful advertising campaigns—the "good life" evokes images of drinking margaritas while lazing on the beach. A life of ease is not equivalent to an actually good life, however.

Instead of these connotations, the good life is what we all want, whether we understand it or not: to strive, to fail, to sometimes succeed, to explore and learn more about our world and ourselves. Aristotle's good life is the examined life of Socrates, in which we live out our values, prioritize correctly, and struggle to accomplish things, sometimes meeting with success, but not always—just to keep us from smugness. At its best, it is a life filled with psychologist Mihaly Csikszentmihalyi's *flow*, by which we fulfill our human potential through work that is its own reward.

The ancient Greek philosopher Epicurus also spent time considering the factors that characterize a good life, and our culture *again* mischaracterizes his advice. While the word "epicurean" now inspires visions of fine dining and fancy wine, Epicurus ate mostly rice. His primary advice for a happy life: avoid pain and spend more time with friends.

Our culture promotes three popular paths to fulfillment: accumulating wealth or prestige, creating a family, and pursuing lifelong learning. A fourth route—far less popular here in the West—is the spiritual pathway, what one might call "un-learning." We all possess unique histories, different agendas, and idiosyncratic hang-ups. None of these pathways is therefore best; rather, we should each choose the path that aligns with our personal contexts and our personalities. Our goals speak to our individuality, but in choosing them, we should keep in mind how much power we might cede to others. For instance, is the desire for wealth rooted in our personal values, or is it actually a social goal—one that we have less control over than we might think? Increased ownership might imply an easier life, but owning more things leads to a corresponding increase in responsibility over them. Your possessions often end up owning *you*. You have to park all those cars and clean all those houses.

*How can we better organize our knowledge?*

Before looking to new sources of data to make our decisions, we should ensure that the data we already have is in proper order. To this end, let's examine the process we commonly use to reach a decision. During our lifetimes, we slowly accumulate knowledge and experience. When faced with a problem, we employ pattern-matching, trying to fit the new situation into a pattern we recognize. When we are sufficiently familiar with things, such as our family or our home, this process is nearly automatic, and we slip into habitual routines without fuss. We even know where to look for information that we do not have; for example, your uncle may be the family record keeper, so you know to consult him on any questions related to genealogy. Despite their limitations, our brains are really quite astounding; more than simple matching machines, they store hierarchies and processes as well. Psychologists call these multistep processes "schemas" and "scripts." When we face a new situation, either we take the necessary time to research an appropriate response, or we match it efficiently to something familiar—which may lead us astray.

Now let us examine the ideal. With a perfect brain, we could store everything that we observe, understand, and know. We would file all of this information under clearly labeled tabs, all accessible by our inner Google. The perfect brain would then sift the results and present us with the best option for any given circumstances. When presented with new information, the perfect brain would continuously reassess its schemas and scripts to keep them up-to-date. Even then, however, the perfect brain would eventually lead us into error, as
236

at best it can only make correct probability assessments.

Let's discuss this perfect brain to determine where the bottlenecks are in the decision-making process—to tell us where we might we fruitfully try to make improvements.

First, we could attempt to improve our memories. However, even were we granted a perfect memory, we would still face an overwhelming number of search results whenever we accessed our knowledge. We file our experiences and knowledge with overlapping tags, be they concepts, visual cues, keywords, place, time, person, etc.—and this is even before considering the emotional content of these memories. Unfortunately, the inner world we live in is quite noisy and chaotic.

Second, we could learn to avoid making mistakes. We could learn the common cognitive biases to keep us from making statistical and logical errors. I highly recommend studying these. Even so, we might still remember things incorrectly, forget them entirely, draw the wrong lessons from our experiences, or react with logic when we should be using use emotion and vice versa.

Third, we could regularly update our ideas, scripts, and schemas. Most of these remain unexamined, let alone up-to-date. Since many are subconscious, psychotherapy is the usual method for examining them; its primary goal—put simply—is to update our outdated behaviors. Candidates for such correction include logically invalid schemas, factually incorrect scripts, and emotionally immature attitudes, to name a few. This process is too idiosyncratic to detail here.

Finally, we could try to improve the filing system itself. Perhaps we could benefit from tagging things more appropriately, or we could revamp the categorization system altogether. Since this method gets so little press, even small changes here could translate into large improvements.

*A whole world of wisdom*

The world of wisdom is very broad. In accordance with this vast reach, this book pulled together knowledge and theories from many disciplines, most notably ecology, philosophy, psychology, and spirituality. Very few people have a reason to sum up this kind of information for you. If you have read this far, I sincerely commend your fortitude and unselfish mentality. Grab your pickaxe and we will climb the unhappy mountain of wisdom together.

*Key Ideas*

- As the universe grows and changes, so does truth.

- Nothing is absolutely good or bad until the universe ends.

- Wise decisions are based on their inputs and intended

- outcomes.

- Every person has a different agenda, whether examined or not.

- Generalists suffer neglect in our culture, but we should welcome them.

- With effort and time, every person can make wiser decisions.

- Wise decisions do not always lead to happiness or wealth.

# a p p e n d i x
# b

## Aligning Values and Goals with Time

When we look at the big picture of our lives, the biggest thing we can observe is how we spend our time—our time is our life in an important sense. How we spend every hour sums up to how we spend our days—which in turn sums up to how we spend our lives. It thus makes sense to look at our time carefully. This appendix looks at hourly time chunks and asks whether our available time lines up with our values and goals. All too often, they do not align.

We must make room in our busy schedules for small pleasures. Small pleasures spread throughout the day are important. The Korean word sohwakhaeng describes such tiny happy moments—like sipping on hot tea or coffee. It is not only the important decisions that ultimately matter. But, here we will look at bigger issues. There are other books that explain time management well, but it is an important enough topic to repeat. Sometimes we neglect important things because we are not managing our schedules well. First, we analyze how we spend our time. Second, we look at our values and goals. Third, we try to align these so that we spend our time doing the things we find important.

**Step 1: Block Out Your Time**

Please pull out some paper and a pencil to draw a grid. Orient the paper so that the longer direction is horizontal. In the leftmost column, mark out twenty-four slots—one for each hour of the day. Start at the top with the hour you typically wake up. Along the top of the paper, make seven columns for the days of the week. If you work Monday through Friday, you should start with Monday.

Our physical and mental health is usually best with roughly eight hours of sleep. Shade in the boxes that correspond with your sleep schedule. This removes about a third of our lives! We cannot change this.

Now mark the times when you are working. Anything that takes effort is work. This is typically another large chunk of time. Obviously if you do not enjoy your job, this is the most important area to focus on.

Block out your remaining hours by writing in what you do during each hour. You might need certain treats, but you might be surprised how much time you waste. This sheet of paper shows how you currently prioritize the things in your life. You might need to change your priorities if they do not reflect your values.

## Step 2: Write Down Your Values

On a new sheet of paper, start listing your values. Try to think of at least five. Values include deeply personal things you want to embody like: courage, honesty, how you want to treat your friends and family, or how you want to be remembered in your obituary. If you have trouble thinking of your values, ask yourself what job you would work if money were no object. Also, what kinds of things did you value when you were ten or twelve years old? Who did you want to be and why? What quirks did you have before you found out that society did not similarly value those things?

Now use these values to examine your time graph from Step 1. You might have to change some things, so that things become better aligned.

## Step 3: Make Two More Lists

Now that you have some ideas about your time and values, we will look at goals and gratitude. Make two separate lists. The first list is things you already have that you wouldn't give up for a million dollars. (If you are a millionaire, change the number to a billion.) Be creative. Think of your body, your experiences, or your relationships. The second list are those things in life that you would prefer to get rather than a million dollars. These things might include recognition, certain types of health or wellness, certain relationships, freedom from certain relationships, or other goals. Try to be realistic, you cannot become an immortal ruler of the universe, but you are free to aim high. If you are honest and imaginative, both of these lists will be surprisingly long. Think of at least five things for each, but with patience you might discover fifty, and finally a limitless list.

The first list is your gratitude list. The second list is your goal list. You should devote time and effort toward achieving your goals. Some of them might be quite realistic. Compare and think about these lists in reference to your time. Now get started on some of your new goals.

# appendix
# c

*Workbook for Integrity*

We often hear the word "integrity" on Sunday mornings, but as with many good ideas, we hear something that moves us, but later find ourselves deluged by more pressing concerns. In the rare event that we do hold on to that Sunday spark, we face the problem of knowing where and how to begin real action toward living with integrity.

This workbook can fill the gap—it gives you the knowledge and practical advice for moving beyond Sunday morning. Because this is a workbook, much of the work will depend upon you. I provide a roadmap, but you must drive the route.

The material covered here is largely psychological, but it is not therapeutic—meaning it draws from everyday concerns and not traumatic events. You can utilize the workbook in solitude, but a group setting would be more enjoyable and likely provide a richer experience.

Our first question is, what does "integrity" mean? We already know it has something to do with morality, but as with any important concept, we should probably consult a dictionary for the full story.

The dictionary gives us two definitions of "integrity." First: "the quality of being honest and having strong moral principles; moral uprightness." Second: "the state of being whole and undivided."

## *Discussion Question 1.1*

How are these two definitions similar?

How are they different?

_____

_____

_____

_____

_____

Ponder this for a few moments. Write down any examples or insights you have that you might want to share with a study group later. While we'll provide some ideas later in this appendix, keep in mind that there is no "right" answer.

An important note: whenever there are blank lines in the workbook, please write down your thoughts before reading on, because you might read something that changes your mind, and you will want to see both your "before" and "after" thoughts.

Let us examine the first definition more deeply. The first definition of "integrity" means "moral uprightness." Thus, a person with integrity is a moral person—someone who is honest and principled. The dictionary does not reveal which principles a person must follow, other than honesty.

What is honesty, and why is it the only principle mentioned? "Honesty" is a word we know well. The simplest equivalent word to honesty is "truthfulness," and the opposite of honesty is deceit. We are honest when there is no difference between what we see and what we report, and no difference between what we believe and what we say we believe. As humans, we are fallible and can be wrong (and often are), but we cannot knowingly lie and still maintain our integrity.

We are honest when:

- what we see = what we report
- what we believe = what we say we believe
- what we say = what we do

Children may lie because they do not yet know right from wrong. Adults may lie because they do not care.

However, for the majority of us, life is a gray area that is more complicated than this definition. Can't we stay silent for fear of hurting someone's feelings? Can't we lie in order to "do good"?

List your ideas about whether lying is always bad. Again, this is not a trick question; most of us at least believe in being polite.

## *Discussion Question 1.2*

Is honesty always the best policy?

_____

_____

_____

_____

_____

Let us now turn to the second definition of "integrity": "the state of being whole and undivided." You might notice that this meaning does not mention communication at all, whereas that seemed a major focus of the first definition. So, what does it mean to be whole and undivided? Let's start with a nonhuman example: when a ship's hull has integrity, it will keep the crew safe and not crack. This example deals with *physical* integrity; humans need physical integrity to lead healthy lives. God (or the universe) takes care of this for us until we get sick or injured. When we are healthy, we are more likely to seek the non-physical types of integrity: emotional, spiritual, or social.

"Wholeness" means there are no missing pieces. Most of us feel that things are missing from our lives. This is not necessarily bad, because it motivates us toward improvement. We want peace for the world and for ourselves. We want unity.

What pieces are missing from your life? Can you imagine yourself being whole even if you never obtain these things?

# Discussion Question 1.3

What are you missing from your life that would make you feel complete?

_____

_____

_____

_____

_____

The next part of the definition of "integrity" deals with division. How can a person live undivided? This implies that there are divisions in a person to begin with. Yes, most of us do feel divided, but what exactly does this mean?

## *Discussion Question 1.4*

How do you as a person feel divided?

_____

_____

_____

_____

_____

If you are able to list the ways that you are divided, then you are already on a track toward integrity, because seeing a problem is always the first step to solving it. Humans have felt divided from nature from the moment Adam covered his body with a fig leaf. We exist in skin bags divided from one another. Humans like to divide everything: we divide property and land, we divide our bodies from our minds. Education itself is mostly concerned with dividing things and naming them.

While we cannot solve all these problems, the *internal* divisions we live with are within our abilities to address and improve. In other words, we can address some of our inner psychological divisions. Our lives divide in many ways, and we are pulled in many directions at once. We are pulled variously by the physical, the emotional, the spiritual, the social, the lawful, the vocational, and many other demands. Trying to balance all of our responsibilities is obviously more than a workbook can handle, thus we choose here to concentrate on

252

just a few psychological concepts.

We are undivided when:

- our thoughts and emotions are undivided
- our words and thoughts are undivided

Now, these are different from honesty, because no outsider can judge them. They deal with inner thoughts and thus a kind of inner integrity. Of course, this does not make them any less important, because we spend so much time with ourselves!

We can now see that both definitions hint at two facets of the same thing. We can see that the phrase "things lining up" visually addresses the crux of both definitions.

We have integrity when:

- what we see lines up with that we report
- what we believe lines up with what we say we believe
- what we say lines up with what we do
- our thoughts line up with our emotions
- our words line up with our thoughts

# *Discussion Question 1.5*

Can we always judge another person's integrity?

_____

_____

_____

_____

_____

Sometimes we can judge the existence or lack of a person's outer integrity and sometimes we cannot. We cannot read people's thoughts, and therefore it is nearly impossible to judge someone's *inner* integrity. Of course, we should probably not be judging other people in the first place, unless we have a specific reason to.

Pro tip: *Do not strive for 100 percent integrity. That is impossible for a human. Strive for* more *integrity than you currently have.*

Since the "honesty" portion of integrity is rather self-explanatory, the remainder of this appendix focuses on what it means to align your thoughts with your emotions, and your words with your actions. But before we can align anything, we need to know exactly what it is we are aligning.

Positive psychology, a branch of psychology that studies and promotes human virtues, labels your thought as "cognition" and your emotion as "affect," with the letter *a*, pronounced as in the word "apple."

Your affect varies from positive to negative, but also from low to high intensity—what we call activation. Thus, you could be slightly sad, very sad, slightly joyful, or very joyful. While we can often label our emotions if we sit with them for a while, our cognition is even more complicated. Just as emotions come and go—sometimes within seconds—our thoughts are constantly arising, whether we want them to or not. How could we get these chaotic systems to line up? The first step is merely to observe your emotions and thoughts.

## *Discussion Question 1.6*

What emotions have you felt over the past twenty minutes?

_____

_____

_____

_____

_____

After you have listed some emotions, go back and label them as positive, negative, low intensity, or high intensity. Some emotions are complex and not easily categorized; for example, nostalgia is both positive and negative for most people.

Thoughts are even more complicated and less researched than emotions! How many thoughts do you think you've had in the last twenty minutes? How might you begin to categorize thoughts?

## *Discussion Question 1.7*

How might you categorize the various thoughts you have?

_____

_____

_____

_____

_____

Do your thoughts cause your emotions, or do your emotions cause your thoughts? Actually, there is evidence that the process works in both directions. A smell can cause disgust before a thought arises, then infect your thoughts to call up other things you don't like. Likewise, you can choose to think pleasant thoughts by practicing gratitude for the blessings in your life. Such thoughts would lead to positive emotions.

Most people are able to choose their thoughts more easily than they can choose their emotions. Therefore, if you learn to control your thoughts, you can begin to control your emotions as well. Now you should know something about what integrity means. If you know less than when you started, do not worry—integrity is complicated.

*Review Questions*

- The first meaning of "integrity" is _____.

- The second meaning of "integrity" is _____.

- These two meanings are similar because _____.

- An emotion contains _____ and _____.

- Your thoughts should line up with your _____.

- Your actions should line up with your _____.


*Additional Questions to Ponder:*

- Can animals have integrity?

- How is integrity similar to wisdom? Humility?


*Suggested Activities*

- Meditate on integrity until you fully understand its meaning.

- Practice observing your thoughts and emotions.

- Observe whether your actions line up with your thoughts and emotions.

# a p p e n d i x
# d

## Humor and Wisdom:
## "I Say Tomato, But You Say Tomato"

### Overview

We begin this section with a quote from poet G.K. Chesterton: "Angels can fly because they take themselves lightly." Likewise, there is no wisdom without humor. While worship services can be solemn, we should make room for joy and humor. If we cannot laugh at ourselves, we are not close to wisdom. We must lighten up. That said, humor can also be a negative force, and we will explore that darker aspect as well.

### The positive ends of humor

Centuries ago, the wisecrackers were often the fools—the court jesters—because they were the only ones who could openly mock the monarch. They could speak truth to power, even if obliquely. Today, in their place, we have stand-up comedians. In her comedy set *Nanette*, for example, Hannah Gadsby speaks truth to power through humor. Yes, there is an element of subversion to much humor.

The wisest, most subversive, and longest joke we have in American culture is the movie *Citizen Kane*. The setup lasts more than an hour! If you can enter into the movie's world, the punchline feels more like a stomach punch than a laugh. But it is a joke—the best kind of joke—because it helps us see the world in a new and wiser light. Science fiction movies like *Logan's Run* and *Planet of the Apes* may have similar structures, but they don't take *us* for a ride.

Jerry Seinfeld is probably America's comedian-in-chief. Instead of trivializing the problematic as jesters did, he problematizes the trivial: this woman has "man hands" or this man stands too close to you when he talks. The show is famously "about nothing." Perhaps one day Seinfeld will use his platform for social change. But it is enough for anyone to simply make us laugh.

While Seinfeld can no longer tell a *surprise* joke, he has many other tools, such as inversion. The easiest joke to tell is the inversion of subject and object. For example, Seinfeld tells of a dream he had where a cheeseburger was eating *him*. Here we can also imagine various anthropomorphized animals. Humorist Gary Larson often makes these leaps. For example, on Earth we see the face of the man on the moon. In one of Larson's comics, an alien on another planet is looking at Earth.

This alien is shaped like the American continent. He sees one of his own kind on Earth!

After inversion, we can try displacement—moving the locus of awareness to a new area without directly swapping. You need this outside awareness to create jokes, and you have to be something of a cultural outsider. This outsider status is a more objective perspective than when every little thing matters greatly to you. It may seem self-evident, but if you take the world too seriously, you will not find humor in it.

There are many different levels of humor, but anything that makes people laugh is good enough, from sight gags and slapstick to political satire. The sound of laughter comes from the clashing and smashing of two different worldviews. For example, slapstick happens when the adult worldview meets the child worldview. Puns occur when the literal language meets the mere *sounds* of language. A pun is not just a sound but must also resemble a different word that *should* be totally unrelated but sounds almost identical. Its wisdom is in showing us how language seemingly makes this mistake. Two completely unrelated words should not sound the same in a perfect system.

In one framework, we can judge humor by audience response. Puns elicit groans. Small jokes elicit titters. Great jokes get roars of laughter. Sometimes a joke gets *applause* instead of laughter. What could this mean? That the audience appreciates the effort, perhaps? I think it means that the audience received a dose of wisdom.

Wisdom and humor coincide most in Taoist sage Zhuangzi's writings. Zhuangzi expressed relativity like a postmodernist. He used humor to show the limits of our conceptions. When asked what to do with his body after he died, he replied, "Above, the crows and kites will eat me; below, the mole-crickets and ants will eat me; to take from those and give to these would only show your partiality."

To show how humans projected their desires as if they were truths, he said, "Men claim that Mao-chiang and Lady Li were beautiful, but if fish saw them they would dive to the bottom of the stream, if birds saw them they would fly away, and if deer saw them they would break into a run. Of these four, which knows how to fix the standard of beauty for the world?"

When observing how humans busied themselves and tried to be productive, he said: "Cinnamon is edible, so the cinnamon tree is cut down. Chi oil is useful, so the Chi tree is gashed. On the other hand, a sacred oak, whose wood was good for nothing and accordingly was spared, said to the axman in a dream, "For a long time I have learned to be useless. On several occasions I was nearly destroyed, but I have now succeeded in being useless, which is of greatest use to me. If I were useful, could I have become so great?"

Finally, he takes away all of our assumptions about reality. "Once upon a time, Zhuangzi dreamed that he was a butterfly, flying about enjoying itself. It did not know that it was Zhuangzi. Suddenly he awoke, and veritably was Zhuangzi again. He did not know whether it was Zhuangzi dreaming that he was a butterfly, or whether it was the butterfly dreaming that it was Zhuangzi."

*Consider a tree*

Like Taoism, Buddhism is also fond of using jokes to show wisdom. In one story, Two Buddhist monks spend a quiet afternoon on a lightly forested hillside. Suddenly one of them points to a tall oak and says, "They call that a tree." Both monks erupt into laughter.

Why is this funny to the monks? To observe the intricacies of reality is quite different from the simple process of labeling such things for communication. This anecdote shows our tendency to sum up infinitely complicated materials and processes into a single word. However, the joke is only *funny* because the monks also understand the other perspective—that the word tree *does* convey some sort of information. Had the monks been remarking on some totally alien concept, they would have pondered rather than laughed. The clashing of the different paradigms creates the humor.

In some sense, we can only understand things based on categorization. When we *specify* something, do we describe its unique aspects, or do we explain why it is a member of a certain species? Indeed, when we label an object—in this case, a tree—we claim that it exhibits the patterns of an abstract archetype that only exists in real-life examples. The word "tree" describes both a pattern and a unique instance. We easily recognize this pattern—we know trees whenever we see them. Like snowflakes, they exhibit commonalities yet are never identical. In other words, they form repeating patterns, but not *identical* repeating patterns.

We ask the old oak tree for its wisdom, and it replies:

> *I understand the turning of the seasons. I wait patiently in winter to conserve my energy. In spring, I grow; I reach toward the sun and dig deep for water. In summer, I work my 9 to 5 job. In autumn, I discard the possessions I no longer need. I know which way the wind blows; I cannot move far, so I use the wind to scatter my seeds. Finally, like Queen Victoria, I never expose my lower body. Old habits die hard.*

### The dark side of humor

Humor can be more evil than wise. There are two main negative aspects to humor. First, we can use it to strengthen our ingroup against people who cannot defend themselves. Sometimes we scapegoat people and make fun of them to strengthen our own ingroup or our own ego. When we have more power than the person we are poking fun at, we are showing the opposite of empathy. When we make fun of a person with disabilities, that is not a wise use of humor—or power. Most of us would agree that when we have the upper hand and there is already a power differential between us and the butt of our jokes, the jokes are not very funny. They are merely mean-spirited. It's one thing to poke fun at a leader, and quite another thing to poke fun at a hungry homeless person. I do not recommend making fun of anyone on a personal level, but that call is yours to make.

When we have an ingroup, we define it in part

by naming our outgroup. Inside jokes can mark us as the special ones. Mean-spirited jokes about outsiders are a bit petty. If we are pursuing wisdom, we should be pursuing an ever larger ingroup, as discussed in Chapter 7. Inside jokes and mean jokes about outsiders merely strengthen the exclusionary nature of our group.

Second, we can use humor to deflate a serious situation. There is a longstanding idea that humor works like a pressure valve, releasing the built-up pressure of a system, such as a society. When we dissolve this pressure, we preserve the status quo instead of allowing potentially positive changes to occur. Sometimes a tense situation can be averted by introducing humor. Now, if two people are brawling in a bar, we would perhaps like them to stop. But if a democratic revolution is occurring and the party in power simply wants to diffuse the situation, we might see this effort at humor as negative. What is a game at one level of power becomes a fight for survival at another level.

# About the Author

Robert Stonehill writes at the intersection of empathy, empowerment, and creative thinking. He has spent fifteen years studying academic wisdom and spirituality, influencing theorists across the globe. Formally, he has studied in all three divisions of modern academia—math and science at Harvard, social science at Purdue, and humanities at Reed. In early 2014, he began hosting monthly wisdom workshops in Portland, Oregon.

Read more at **RobertStonehill.com**